T0158980

Trust Me!

A True Story About Friends and Fraud on Facebook

Lisa Larsson

authorHOUSE®

AuthorHouse™
1663 Liberty Drive
Bloomington, IN 47403
www.authorhouse.com
Phone: 1 (800) 839-8640

Published by AuthorHouse 06/19/2018

ISBN: 978-1-5462-4321-2 (sc)
ISBN: 978-1-5462-4320-5 (e)

Library of Congress Control Number: 2018906169

Print information available on the last page.

This book is printed on acid-free paper.

I had recently opened a Facebook account and had not yet a lot of friends. I was curious to see what this social medium could lead to. I am generally interested in other people, as an observer mostly. I am interested in hearing what they say and how they express their thoughts and feelings. I don't want to be surrounded by people in a physical sense all the time, I prefer to be all alone for some periods, and I often prefer writing to talking to people. This medium would open doors to other peoples' lives, I hoped. I was generous to admit all the persons that wanted to be friends with me to my Facebook account. I welcomed everyone who made requests to be friends with me. After some weeks with my Facebook account, I had some friend requests from men I didn't know before. These men were all military persons who worked abroad in some areas where the UN and the American army are operating to protect the inhabitants from intruders, like the IS in Syria and Iraq or the Talibans in Afghanistan. I deleted most of those contacts, as they were too intrusive; one of these men asked me to help him receive money from some services he had done in Afghanistan. It was his future pension, he said. We would meet somewhere and I would hand over the money I had received. I said, "No thank you. I don't want to be involved in money transactions" and deleted him from my list of friends.

One of these military men was Edward Anderson. He was the first and only person I have had an extended acquaintance with without knowing him before. He presented himself as an officer working under cover to protect the inhabitants in Syria from the rebel forces active there. I didn't ask for details about his family, but he spontaneously gave some information about his life situation: he was a Roman Catholic, had a son, his wife had died. His son was twelve years, a student at a boarding school. He said he would sometimes burst into tears when he thought of his late wife. He and his colleagues were there to protect the Syrians, thereby risking their own lives. I expressed my admiration for this assignment. I returned some information about myself. I told him I am fortunate enough to be married to a man who loves me, though we have quite different interests. Our common interests are nature and animals, that's why we live in the countryside. My husband likes to care for his forest, planting trees, having trees felled and chopped into wood for our fireplace. I had no plans to start a kind of romantic affair, I was just curious to know more about the environment where he was staying, to learn something about the Syrians' living conditions during this terrible war going on there. What were he and his colleagues doing for them? How did they cope with the situation? How is a military camp organized?

I never received much information about his life in the camp though, not while he was staying there. Edward didn't give away any secrets about his military life. Later, when he was staying in London, he said that he had seen on TV the location where his camp had been, and he then felt sorry for those who still were there, because they were staying very close to the place where there had been clashes. Some months later, when he had returned home, he said, "I just want to live peacefully with my son in my house. That period in the camp has done harm enough in my life." On one occasion, he said something about the rebels that he and his fellows had been fighting against in Syria. "They have very powerful weapons and they are very intelligent but they will not outsmart us, we are more intelligent, you can be sure of that". "I hope so", I answered. But I wasn't sure who was on the "right" side in this war. The Syrian war is difficult to analyze for anyone who is not interested in politics. In all honesty, I was not sure which side the American soldiers supported, al Assad's or the Turkish side? The rebels belong to different groups. All I knew was that the war had been going on for many years and it seemed never to end. I was keen to hear about the country that so many young people come from, seeking asylum in my country. I have met many young Syrians while working as a guardian.

We exchanged some very trite and harmless words every day while he was in the Syrian camp. He would give some jaunty citations about being positive and full of go. "Winners are no quitters, quitters are no winners"– something like that. I used to give some information about what happened in Sweden at that time. I told him that the pope was visiting Sweden, which was a great event since we are Protestants in our country. This visit would symbolize the atonement between Protestants and Catholics. I told him about the Euro Cup of Women's Handball that was going on, and sometimes I told him about my work with young asylum seekers. Edward gave no more than commonplace comments to whatever I informed him of. "That's nice" and similar phrases was all he said. No more profound remarks. He often asked if I had eaten and I told him what kind of food I had eaten. He never commented on that either. I asked him if the food he received tasted good, and he answered, "Not really".

His questions to me concerned mostly how my night was or if I had eaten anything. The conversation was hardly ever more sophisticated than so. I presumed he wanted to know if I had slept well, nothing more intimate than that. When I answered I had not eaten anything, because I had no appetite, he urged me to eat something. I answered, "OK. I will".

I am the youngest of three children. My sister is thirteen years older and grew up mainly with her maternal grandparents. My three-year-older brother and I grew up in an ordinary family in a big city. We lived in a society that was characterized by the social welfare that was the hallmark of the Social Democratic Party's politics. The times were changing from a traditional class society to a more equalized society where higher education became increasingly a natural choice for anyone who wanted to move on to higher education after high school. My brother studied technology at the university and became a civil engineer. My favorite subjects at school were humanities: history, psychology, Latin, German, French. When my high school time was finished, I started studying languages at the university. I had no clear idea of what profession these studies would lead to, but I imagined that I would most likely end up as a teacher. I enjoyed my years of university studies; if it wasn't for the scarcity of money I could have been a perpetual student. My first professional experiences as a teacher were however less than pleasant. It was then hard to get a permanent, good job in the district where I lived. After some years as a supply teacher at different schools, I was fed up with this kind of work. I resumed my studies at the university, this time at a postgraduate level, and took my doctor's degree in Nordic languages. Since then, I have largely taught at college level.

I have taken an active interest in helping young asylum seekers that have come to Sweden. I have been a guardian for some boys and one girl from different countries without parents in Sweden, unaccompanied minors. All boys and girls below eighteen years are considered to be children, and are relatively well taken care of. After their eighteenth birthday, they are in a legal sense adults, and are supposed to manage on their own. Being a guardian, *god man* in Swedish, means that you help these children with their lives in different respects, for example their contacts with authorities, health care and school. During the autumn of 2015 more than 35,000 unaccompanied minors came from war zones like Syria, Somalia, Iraq and Afghanistan to Sweden. I found the work with these young people important and rewarding. Our society is quite different from the societies in the countries these young people come from. The languages they speak are also totally different. Because of the cultural differences between our countries, there will of course be misunderstandings on both sides in the communication. It is necessary to book an interpreter via phone to be able to talk to them during their first months in Sweden, and it was mostly difficult to get this service because of the great demand for interpretation into the languages these young people speak. Sometimes there were technical problems with the loudspeakers or the quality of the translations. It is difficult to translate the words that denote typical phenomena for our culture from Swedish into Somali, Dari, Arabic and other languages in a way that makes the communication effective. My work with these young people boosted my interest in the countries they come from. This interest in other countries was the reason why I had engaged in a conversation with Edward in the first place. In my ordinary work as a senior lecturer and professor I get in touch with people from all walks of life, several of them are future high school teachers and quite a few have their origin in other countries than Sweden. Communicating with a soldier in an area where some of the young people come from was perceived as a natural connection to my regular work.

A CALL FOR HELP

After some weeks Edward started his daily conversation with a call for distress, "I need your help." I was astonished and shocked at the same time. He had seemed to be so cheerful before! I waited some time before I responded, "What kind of help do you need?"

"I've been seriously injured I don't want to die here you can help me get away from here"

"You should be helped by the Army or the Red Cross."

"There is a lot you don't know about the Army you don't leave until mission done."

"You should ask relatives or close friends instead of me."

"Do you think I would have asked you, if I had? You can write a letter to the Recess Department you tell them you are a friend of mine, and that you want to help your friend to get home."

"Write a letter – yes, that's something I can do."

"It costs some money to ask for leave I can't pay that now I have no access to my bank account but I will pay back as soon as I return home I'm not poor, trust me."

"How much?"

"Something like 1300-1500 euros."

When I heard about the amount of money needed to apply for leave, I was very reluctant to go on with this. I am used to living within small frames economically, I have always had to be careful with the money I have earned. I have tried to save money for my old age, and have invested some money in share funds. To give away first 1,500 euros and some days later another 4,500 euros was a great sacrifice, even if I, at that point, was confident that I would get back the money. I had to make withdrawals from different accounts, sell some shares to gather all the 6,500 euros. I had never before bought anything that cost more than 4,500 euros.

All kinds of thoughts and feelings went through my head, and I had the feeling this could be something very risky, my future would be destroyed if I was mistaken about the man's honesty. How would I ever be capable to cope with such a mistake? Could I forgive myself, if it would turn out he was just a common deceiver? He had no reason to expect me to sacrifice for him – we had never met personally, and we had just exchanged some small talk through Facebook's Messenger. But I believed that he was in a very troublesome situation, being severely injured, though not so dangerously as he had implied, I guessed. He needed to be helped by someone. He sent a snapshot showing him lying on the floor with a wounded leg. There must be someone in the camp who was able to help him? He said there was no one to help him in his vicinity. Now and then he would write, "I have to take my medication now". Probably he had some aching wound, and he was given some painkillers to take at intervals.

He used so many pleading phrases to arouse my compassion. I cannot tell how many "please" he sent, he used this word in practically all sentences. The "sentences" were not marked with dots or any graphic signs except for some question marks sometimes to indicate a question, "Eaten?"

I went for a long walk when I was asked to pay for Edward's journey home. I was scared to empty all my accounts. My savings amounted to scarcely 10,000 euros if I used up all the small amounts of money I had. But I couldn't stop thinking of the desperate "please, please help me" that he had sent to me. I felt somehow this must be done, I had to raise the money. I would feel happy when he was free to go home, and he would soon pay back, wouldn't he? Nothing would happen to me, no one would know anything about this transaction if it was finished within a few weeks. My husband would know nothing about this "affair". I would be compensated for all the trouble I had and all the anxiety I might have before Edward had paid back.

When I told Edward that I would pay the money for his journey home, he said he would write the letter I was formally to sign and send to the Recess Department. This is a department within the UN, Edward told me, which has the task to help officers like him in difficult situations. I did not question the information he gave me. I don't know anything about military organizations and very little about the organization of the United Nations. It sounded reasonable that there was something like the Recess

Department, though I never had heard about it. Edward formulated a letter that I would direct to the Recess Department. He returned to me some hour after I had agreed to give him help to get leave from his service in Syria. I started my correspondence with this department about the money transactions. The short letters from Vacation Department were mostly not signed by a specific individual, only on very few occasions there was a name of an individual at the bottom of the page. I was asked to transfer the money to a private person, who reportedly was an agent of the Recess Department. The name of the receiver of the first transaction was Maria MacMillan, a name that resurfaced later, when I was contacted by the teacher and mentor of Edward's son. She had the same name as this receiver. I later saw that this combination of a given name and surname is not uncommon in the U.S.

I read the letter Edward had written, which was a mixture of pompous and casual style, with no special punctuation marks between "sentences". I signed with my name at the bottom.

When I contacted a money transfer company, I found warnings against sending money to people you never have met personally. "Never send money to a person you have not met" they said. This warning made me tremble and reconsider my decision to transfer money to the person I had been referred to as a receiver. I was in anguish when I defied the warnings and went on in the process of transferring money. I also had a call from an official of the company, she asked me some questions about the purpose of this transaction, and admonished me to be very careful. There are so many people who say they are in a desperate situation and need help, but they just want to get hold of your money, she said.

I learned a new concept for the situation of being persuaded to give money by someone who deceives you – *scam*. In Merriam-Webster's dictionary the definition of this word is: 'a fraudulent or deceptive act or operation, e.g. an insurance scam'. The origin of the word is not known. Scam is similar in form to the word spam for email that mostly is unsolicited advertising. The first time the word was used in this sense was 1963. The crime itself has probably been committed for as long as humans have existed, but through Internet it has increased and become more sophisticated than before, more difficult to recognize as fraud and also to take legal measures against. A more specific word that is used for this crime is *confidence trick*. According to Wikipedia a confidence trickster exploits characteristics of the human psyche, such as credulity, naïveté, compassion, vanity, irresponsibility, and greed.

I told Edward that those who administered my money transfers had warned me against him. He assured me he was not one of those unscrupulous persons. "I am a man of discipline, I would commit suicide if I couldn't pay back", he said. He used many words to persuade me to think of him as an honest man. He just didn't have access to his bank account where he was. I paid the 1,685 euros for the letter that would make it possible for him to be released from his service in Syria and go home by air.

The Recess Department sent me a letter where they gave me information about their mission and their purpose to help important military personnel. Their organization is allegedly a secret service of the Department of Peacekeeping Operations, which was of importance later in my correspondence with political authorities. The letter made a very trustworthy impression on me. Edward was an important person, according to the contents of these messages.

. . . .

Madam this is the UN Secret Service of "DPKO" and we are bond with the some special responsibilities which is to secure permissions for Urgent release order for high influence soldiers with extreme responsibilities and extreme intelligence to Service in the UN peacekeeping mission across the world, and with a long period of time of assignment to the location of Service. DPKO also provides guidance and support on military, political and peace building missions.

. . . .

You are hereby required to send some vital details of this soldier in question for clear investigation and proper check of all military details and services data vis-a-vis all military tolerance, discipline and intelligence to services over there in Syria."

They asked me to give this information about Edward: 1. Military Rank. 2. Full Names, 3. Department in Syria. 4. Uniform number. Edward furnished me with the information needed.

Since this was the first time I used this way to make money transactions, I was worried the money would not arrive with the receiver on time. But I was reassured by an official at the Recess Department on this point:

Hello Madam

How are you doing? we shall email you as soon as the receiver receives the payment and immediately after that we shall book the flight for the following day after payment is received and then he would fly, you do not have anything to worry about madam the Vacation has already been approved. Thanks

Sincerely,

1,700 euros is more or less what a one-week holiday trip costs. I used to save money for my holidays and all unforeseen expenses, like repair works on the house, medical treatment beyond the ordinary things covered by the general assurance we have. I have been working as an associate professor at a university for more than twenty years. My salary was about 4,500 euros a month. When income tax is excluded, the remaining sum is about 2,700 euros, which is enough for me to live a good life, I could even set aside 50-60 euros for different charitable organizations every month. I could live a comfortable life with no more excesses than I desired.

The next time I heard from Recess Department they affirmed that they had performed the assignment regarding Anderson's leave of absence, but they would need another 4,500 euros for a ticket with a special plane ("for security reasons") and a ticket for Anderson's stand-in from Jakarta to Syria. I was shocked to hear about this and I protested they had not given me information about this before. If I wanted to back out from this they would pay back the money I had paid, they answered.

I was given two different bank accounts into which I should make deposits, the first one was for Anderson's journey home, and the account holder was someone in Ghana, the second, concerning the trip for the stand-in from Jakarta to Syria, was someone with an Indonesian bank.

Ghana sounded strange to me, reminding me of notorious "Nigeria letters". When I revealed my suspicions to Edward he said it was not phony in any way; he had been flown by a bullet proof plane from Ghana on his trip to Syria. But when I tried to make this transaction, I was contacted by the credit company again, an official calling from Lithuania asked me about the receiver, told me it was probably a case of fraud, and this time they refused to make a transaction. They paid back all the money. Though I was upset and truly uncertain, I asked the Recess Department what other bank account I could use. They then gave me a private bank account in a bank in Turkey. The account holder was allegedly one of their agents.

A new period of worrying thoughts started. I could never relax from this "business", but I had to put up a calm front to all other people around me. I didn't want to get my husband involved in the whole thing, because he is extremely cautious about almost everything. "Mission would be done" within a few days, possibly a couple of weeks, I thought. No one would notice anything. My husband would not be worried without cause. If he knew I had lent money of this size to anyone, he would be furious, in particular if it was a person not known by me before. I had to gather money from different accounts to be able to pay the second amount. Some money had been invested in bank funds and was not available right away. I had to wait some days before I could make the transaction.

Edward was very impatient to learn if I would pay, if I had received a confirmation of the transfer, and he asked if the money had arrived with the Recess Department. I got numerous text messages where he asked about the money. I felt extremely stressful, and I had to put my cell phone on soundless most of the time, since I didn't want my husband or anyone else in my vicinity to ask about the frequent signals from Messenger. I was thrilled by the signals, I even feared the signals as if I were stalked by this man. I felt calm only when I knew the money was paid and could tell Edward that it was on its way to the Recess Department, when I had sent a receipt of the transaction. Edward thanked me many times, saying that God would bless me, that I was the queen of his heart, that people like me were rare. Still I did not feel happy or calm when he talked like that. I was more inclined to feel a heavy press on my shoulders; his wishes were like a millstone around my neck. I wanted to get rid of the mission to pay for his freedom from military service as soon as possible. I promised myself I would do some nice things when the money was paid back.

I am hardened enough by my experiences from other men and women to realize that this American was not really my friend, he didn't know me well enough to feel more than gratitude for my help. He addressed me with "dearest" in his text messages, which I found acceptable and not too intimate. On a few occasions, he called me "my love" or "honey" but he stopped doing this when he learned I didn't fancy him as a lover. I told him very early that I was fortunate enough to have a husband who loves me, even though we have different interests. Sometimes Edward asked what my husband was doing or he asked me to send pictures of me and my family and the children I have taken care of, but I never did so. I told him that for integrity reasons I could not send pics of other people than myself. I sent however some snapshots of my cats. He didn't seem to appreciate these pictures though. His comment would be "nice" and the like.

I had some problems when I tried to raise the money that was needed. I checked several times how much more I needed. There were 4,400 euros when I had included the fee the bank charged for the transaction. Some 200 euros were missing and I was pressed to get it done as quickly as possible. I felt a constant press from Edward's messages. I had to choose the Express variant of transmissions, because it was so urgent that the money should arrive as fast as possible. The Recess Department would do nothing at all before they had received the money. I felt extremely nervous during the time I was planning the transaction, carrying out the job with the bank, and waiting for a confirmation on my display. I checked dozens of times if the transaction had gone through, and I waited for a message from the Recess Department that they had received the money and would set about the whole thing.

When the money had been transferred to the person that the Recess Department had entered as a receiver (a Turkish name), they sent a kind of diploma that contained some data about Anderson's service for the Department for Peacekeeping Operations. It was, I presume, intended as a proof for me to see that Anderson had done something important for the army. I found the language clumsy; two words were wrongly spelt and the sentences were not marked correctly. The signature made by the Chief of the Army staff was not legible.

The words *approved* ('*apporved*') at the bottom of the paper and *endeavor* ('*endevor*') were spelt wrongly in this document, the word *furore* was probably meant to be *future*. The word might be an interference phenomenon from the Italian language, it does not belong to Standard English. The phrase "Good luck in your future endeavors" is sometimes used when someone has been released from his/her job. The noun phrase "extreme honor" ("I want to thank you for your extreme honor") does not fit in well in the text. There should have been a dot to mark the end of the main clause after *8 months*. Would this imperfect English be good enough for a diploma from a chief of the army? I reacted against the language style, but I was not sure my reaction was justified. I have seen many bombastic texts written by people whom you expect to be capable writers. At that point I was indulgent towards style and grammar mistakes. I was a bunch of nerves and felt somehow dizzy all the time. I didn't allow myself to think in a critical way, I didn't have the power to say "NO. This is absurd!" I was both kind and stupid. I felt I had already entered an enterprise that could or should not be broken off, when I once had offered help. I was walking on very thin ice that at any point would break and pull me down to the bottom. While I liked the thought of saving someone, I was at the same time terrified when I thought of the misery that this could bring to me. Being destitute of money means for me a total disaster, even if I live in a country that offers some basic security for all their citizens. But I would not ask for community help, unless I were in deep distress.

I never felt more than sympathy for Edward. He sounded genuine when he talked about his situation. He seemed to appreciate my talk about my life and what was going on in Sweden. He was polite in his way of talking to me, but at the end of our acquaintance he sometimes was annoyed with me. The conversation became less cordial when he realized I wouldn't help him more. Beside the small passport photo he sent while in London, I have no picture of him, and I never asked him to describe himself. I endeavored to be quite strict but kind in my way towards him. He, on the other hand, squandered a lot of praise on me for being so kind, so extraordinarily kind and honest. He said he would remunerate me later when he had returned home. "I won't disappoint you", he said.

I had no romantic ideas about officers as being particularly grand, gentlemanlike. But I did believe that his rank represented something of discipline and honesty. I have no friends nor relatives who serve in the army. There used to be mandatory military service for all fit young men in Sweden. They were "mustered" at the age of 18 years. The army is now based mainly on professional soldiers, but it has proved difficult to attract young men and women to the military profession. In recent years, they have reintroduced military service for young men and women who of their own will want to do military service for some months. My husband and my son did their military services after high school, both being anything but positive to military life. People in general have a negative attitude to the army and to those who work for the army. The words *military* and *obedience* are no words of prestige nowadays, you don't connect military life with "thinking freely, in a critical way", which is cherished as the ideal in our modern society. The hierarchy of military life does not agree with the democratic way of ruling that is common in work and education system in our society. It was actually a kind of challenge for me to be befriended to a military man. I had some prejudices against this category of men.

When I had made the financial transactions needed for his journey home to Baltimore, there were some days when I felt relieved, I felt I had done my duty. But I received so many worried messages from Edward about this, that I became anxious about it all again. He would send lots of questions about the money: "Have you heard from your bank? How long will it take before they receive the money? Have you sent a receipt of the money transaction to the Recess Department?"

When he some days later got the confirmation that he would be allowed to return home he wrote "I am so very very happy". Lovely to hear for me! He received a ticket for the flight, and the day before his flight home he had a long talk with his commander. He sent a message to me about this: "The commander gave me a sealed box that he wants me to hand over to his wife when I arrive in the U.S. I asked him what the contents were, and he answered 'it's our family fortune'. What is in the box, do you think?"

"It sounds fishy", I answered. "You should demand he open the box and show you the contents. What could happen to you if the airport officials find there is something illegal in the box?"

Edward was feeling uneasy about this box, but he also seemed to have great respect for his superiors. He said he would ask the other officers about this. He asked me about my telephone number and my email address, that he would use when he arrived home.

TROUBLES IN LONDON – CUSTODY AND TRIAL

The flight was due on November 4, but he would make a stopover in London before the flight to Baltimore. This day I was busy on my work and I turned off my phone for several hours to not be bothered by telephone calls or messages on Messenger. I was worried he would call me too often when he got home, that he thought that I would somehow invite him to have a close friendship, maybe visit me in my home. I was keen to finish the acquaintance, or at least keep it at a very modest level. Maybe I could send some short messages now and then, if he wanted to keep our friendship alive.

When I was leaving my office to go home I saw I had missed telephone calls from Great Britain, two or three times. I expected to find a message that confirmed that Edward had returned home safely, or at least was on his way back home. There was however a text message from him saying, "I am finished my love, the box from the commander was scanned, it contained a lot of 100-dollar bills. I have been taken into custody, please call me as soon as possible." My immediate reaction was anger mixed with disappointment. I didn't feel sorry for him, rather I was furious since I at that moment feared that this was a case of fraud. My early misgivings turned out to be justified. I feared he tried to entangle me into something very troublesome and costly. I sent a text message to him while still being very angry, "What a mess! I think you have exploited our short Facebook friendship in an outrageous way! Don't harass me more! I must work." I had hoped so very much to get back what I had invested into his leave from the military service! What would this lead to? Was Edward co-working with some other phony men, was this a real scam that the bank officials had warned me against? I was very upset. I regretted having offered him help from the start.

Later that evening I got another text message from Edward, "Why are you condemning me so fast? i brought the box the commander gave me, i didn't know the contents. i will be executed".

"You have put yourself in a very troublesome situation", I answered. He answered with two question marks. "You are however in a country where they speak English, and you are entitled to legal help. They will treat you humanely", I declared.

"Who told you they don't have anyone killed here?"

"The last time they had a person executed in Great Britain was in the sixties. If you are innocent, you have nothing to fear. I can help you no more. NO MORE FEES".

Edward was upset with my harsh tone, "why do you talk like the law to me? you know what happened."

Later he asked me to contact a certain Geofrey Nelson by writing a letter to him. He gave me an email address to Nelson.

"Who is Nelson and what can he do for you?", I asked.

"He is a lawyer. He can come and talk with me. Tell him everything that happened"

"Okay, I will do that". Writing a letter didn't cost anything.

I am mostly quick to do errands. I immediately wrote an email letter to Geofrey Nelson where I explained the situation about Edward.

I was in a state of despair and rage because of this turn of the affair. I despaired I would ever get those 6,500 euros back and it was a hard blow for me. Would I ever forgive myself for spending 6,500 euros on something so risky for someone I didn't know well? And now he had the nerve to ask for more help. He expected me to react as if I were his wife or a sister.

I have always been careful not to spend more money than I can afford. Now I would have to be stingy towards myself and to those I care for. Every month I donate some hundred crowns for charitable ends like Save the Children, WWF and to the Organization for the conservation of Nature. I have done so for many years and my intention was never to stop supporting them during my lifetime.

The lawyer Geofrey Nelson visited Edward in the custody. Edward told me later that Nelson had asked him about everything. A lot of detailed questions.

When I received the messages from barrister Nelson, I was astonished that he used such a sloppy English in his answers to me, no full stops at all, no capitalization of names, some wrongly spelt words and some words that were missing, which made the texts to some parts incoherent. This is a style you normally find in text messages from people with a low education, or people who are in a great hurry when they are writing. But this was also characteristic of all the other English-speaking persons I got in touch with around Edward.

Edward made several spelling mistakes and expressed himself in a way that mostly was less than elegant. His texts were bits of spontaneous chat. He sent several different sets of words during one session of talk. That made his messages very similar to spoken words during a conversation. He didn't censor or correct the messages before sending them. Homophonic words were often spelt in the wrong way: *there* was used for *their, some* was used incorrectly for *sum.* Some of these mistakes could be excused as common slips of the pen, that most people do when they text messages, me included. But the tendency was more pronounced than so. He also made many grammar mistakes, or rather – he used the forms used in casual spoken language: She *don't* know; *I dunno* 'I don't know'; *i dint* 'I didn't'.

I don't expect adult persons to be good at writing, I know most people aren't, in particular not when writing private messages. But you expect persons with a long education to be able to spell correctly and be decently good at the grammar of their own mother tongue. I was surprised to find so many clumsy phrases in the lawyer's letters:

"I have contacted the London security service and I am find out what really happened so I would know what and what to do to get him out. Thanks Barrister Nelson".

Later he sent a message where he gave some information from the investigation he had made, which made it clear for me that the sealed box was a case of money laundering, which the commander however had denied being involved in. He said he would be able to make Anderson released from his custody, but this process would cost 26,800 euros, because of the documents he needed. His own charge was 500 euros.

I was shocked to hear the legal process would cost so much, and I asked Nelson why this was so. I wanted Mr. Nelson to give me some concrete information about Edward, but he gave no specific details about Edward's street address. I expressed my doubts about Anderson's character in my mail to him:

Hello █████

Thanks for this information, though it was hardly nice news. I have invested the sum of 6,300€ to help Mr █████ get the Vacation, which has strained my economy severely. I was hoping to get back this money when █████ returned home. So he promised me eagerly. I think it was really unwise to take that box from the commander, which I told him was phoney. (I take it █████ tells the truth, that he has not made it up). I cannot possibly assist him by giving more money to this. Are you sure ██████████ is an honest man? The sums you mention seem to be extremely high.

I would like to have █████ postal address in the US.

Sincerely,
Lisa
(Your name is spelt with 2 f?)

I noted he spelt his name sometimes with one, sometimes with two f's. In his email address the name was spelt with one f, in his letters he used two f's. He answered that the correct spelling should be Geoffrey, with 2 f's. His mother had spelt the name with one f, that's why he sometimes used this form.

He gave some explanation to why it cost so much but it was not really satisfying to me. There were so and so many judges that he had to ask for their signatures, he said. I also asked him if he believed in Anderson's story about the box and what he thought about his character. He answered that Edward's story checked out. He finished the letter by giving a hint that I should help him, though the hint was not explicitly made, the last sentence was "chopped".

Hello madam,

Yes from my investigation mr █████ is an honest man he has said the truth I spoke with him and he told me you

helped him out of Syria I have also contacted the Recess
Department and they confirmed it

. . . .

I felt so bad for your friend because this case is serious and
in United Kingdom security personals are very strict. So if
you could do your best for him better,

The information about Anderson's property was alarming for me.
He didn't own a house or an apartment, and he had a lot of bills! Nelson
expressed himself in a vague and sometimes faulty way, I didn't fully
understand the whole meaning of his letter. I usually scrutinize all texts
to see what information there is in the text and what it indirectly could
mean. This has been part of my profession for so many years. It seems I
feared the truth, I had been so entangled in this "story" that I had lost my
sound judgement.

Could I really trust Geoffrey Nelson? Or was he co-operating with
Anderson in a fraud, to drain me of all my money? Was the whole thing
just a dirty trick? This story about the sealed box from the commander was
a bit odd to me. Why did an officer with long professional experience take
the risk of bringing a sealed box into his luggage? He might have agreed
to bring the box to the U.S., if he would receive a certain reward in return
for the risk.

I never trusted Edward or Mr. Nelson at 100%, that's why it strained my
nerves so much the whole time this business lasted. I can testify to the well
experienced circumstance that uncertainty often is worse than knowledge
of something bad. What did Nelson mean I should do by "doing my best"
to help Edward? Well, he most certainly wanted me to raise a lot of money
for the legal process. I couldn't understand why the process had to cost
money beside the lawyer's fee. Are the judges paid to sign documents in
the U.K.? The lawyer's fee was okay, but the cost for the documents was a
mystery to me. I thought such procedures were paid by public funds like
it is in Sweden.

I was extremely reluctant to give Edward more loans. I reminded him,
using harsh words, of his duty to pay back to me, if there was any honesty
at all with him. I gave him all the information he would need to pay back.

One of these days while Edward was in custody he told me he had all the information that was needed for withdrawals from his bank account. I was given the bank account number of an Indonesian bank where Edward had his bank savings. He gave me his password to open the account and instructed me to make withdrawals to myself and to the lawyer. I logged in to his account and saw that there was a substantial amount of money, almost 400,000 dollars, large enough and more to cover the expenses I had had for him. I did what was needed to make a withdrawal, but I failed to get a receipt of the withdrawal. The transaction was never successfully completed.

When Edward later was in touch with me, he told me that the bank had sent a message to him, saying that no other person than himself could make withdrawals. Since the bank account had been dormant for a long time, he had to visit a bank office and fill in a special form to make the means available. It was obvious that Edward wanted to make me believe in his capacity to pay back what I had spent on his journey home. I was again very disappointed. For some hours, I had been feeling so well, because I believed I would be compensated for my expenses. This roller-coaster between hope and despair was extremely stressful for me.

Edward went on asking for my financial support the next days and weeks. I had to repeat the same message for him several times: I do not have a fortune to pay this huge sum of money that was demanded. He called me a savior, he suggested I ask my friends for a loan, but I told him I have neither wealthy friends nor relatives to ask. And even if I had, I would never ask them for money. I don't even ask my husband for money, we have separate economies but share all the bills and expenses for living. Borrowing money from other people is just impossible for me. It has always been important for me to be economically independent, even towards my husband. Edward then suggested I take a bank loan, which I immediately dismissed as impossible. I take a pride in having no bank loans any more. That's why I had so solid an economy.

Edward was absent from Messenger for a week or so, probably because I had such a staunch attitude to his begging for more money. One day when I had answered his standard phrase "How are you doing?" with my repeatedly told utterance that I have no more money to lend to you, he said "Why are you so harsh with me? I had a bit of good news to tell you." When I asked him what this good news was, he said his son's teacher Maria MacMillan had offered to lend to him almost the whole sum needed for the legal process. Could I contribute with the little balance of 2,600 euros?

I almost automatically said no, but afterwards I brooded on this sum that now sounded so small, even if it was much more than the 1,685 euros I had lent him the first time – after careful deliberation. If I helped him and somehow raised more money, he would be able to go home and pay back the money he owed me. That boosted my endeavor to help him financially. I could do something good for him and at the same time make it possible for myself to get back the money I had spent on him.

He sounded very desperate to be released from the custody. His son was extremely worried he said. It was difficult for me to dismiss him. He used all the means that were available to remind me of his wishes. He often used God in his pleas to me. He didn't use this kind of reference to God, when he later returned to his home in the U.S.

"Please Lisa, I do not know what else to do. Please, you are just my savior, please. I beg you with GOD ALMIGHTY"

Nowadays, it is not common to use phrases like *God bless you, God willing* and the like, unless you are an active religious person, which relatively few people are in Sweden. I have only heard such words being used by the very few fervent believers I have met in my life. These believers belong mostly to "free churches" outside the earlier state-supported church. Church and state are separated since 2003, but the former state church is the one I visit when I sometimes go to church. It is a Lutheran high church with some fixed rituals for their services.

I had three credit cards, which I used only on some rare occasions. If I used the credit given to them I could easily find the 2,600 euros that remained to pay for the documents that would make Nelson capable to have Anderson released. I told him I would try to raise the money, and he was of course grateful. He said he would pay back immediately when he had returned home. He even promised to give some extra money for my patience and honesty to him. I said I wanted no more money back than I had lent to him. If he wanted to show his gratefulness in some way, he could do so by donating money to charitable organizations like Save the Children, World Wildlife Organization or Red Cross.

I had to use my credit cards to get more cash, and then to make deposits into the account that was used to make money transfers abroad. Nowadays the banks don't accept the management of cash, you have to go to some cities where they have those special ATM's for deposits of money. In the next town where I usually do all my errands, there was no such ATM. I had to go to another town to make deposits. There was also one such ATM in the city where I had my work, which I sometimes used. But I could only make withdrawals of 5000 crowns (equal to 500 euros) at the most for a time period of seven days. If I used both credit cards I could raise 2,600 euros. These financial errands were a new experience to me. I had never had to deal with cash like this before: making withdrawals from one ATM and then immediately go to another town with a more advanced ATM to make deposits into my other bank account. I felt like a very desperate victim of extortion that I have seen in some movies. What added to this feeling was the fact that I had to do it without arousing suspicion from my husband that I was in a troublesome situation. I had to keep up appearances that everything was okay, even if I was close to breaking down. I sometimes regretted that my husband was unable to "read" the behavior of people in a good way, now I was grateful he was so gullible. I had to do errands of this sort many times, but I always managed to give reasonable explanations as to why it was such a hurry to do them.

I contacted Geoffrey Nelson to ask him about his bank account, and he gave me a bank account in a German bank belonging to another person. Why didn't he want me to make a deposit into his own bank account in a British bank? This might indicate that there was something phony about this business. They –the Recess Department and the lawyer– both secret ways to receive money. This arrangement indicated that their activity wasn't completely legal business.

RELEASE FROM CUSTODY
AND MORE TROUBLES

T he day when Edward was to be tried before the court, he asked me to pray for him. During the first months of our acquaintance he often referred to God in his language, as is common in the American culture. He asked on two occasions to pray for him. I told him I am not a strong believer but I would pray for him. I'm not a religious person, but I pray to God at night before falling asleep. Maybe it is wishful thinking to believe that there is a God who listens to us and who more or less rules our lives. I hope there is a good power helping us in some way. Later that day I got email from the lawyer, a message that Anderson now was released, but Edward had not been allowed to leave his custody, since he had incurred some debt to the custody because of his using Internet and some extra feeding. His debt was almost 3,500 euros. Could I pay this for him?

"Hello Madam good morning, the case today was a success and Mr Edward is now free to depart London [...].

the warder at the prisons informed me he has a bill of 3460 euros which he must pay before he departs I was told he quested for internet access and also his extra feeding."

Not again! I was upset about this asking for more money. But I could not abandon him now, when he had almost one foot in the plane to Baltimore, could I? Edward asked me to give him another loan to pay his debt, a new flight ticket, some extra money for taxi and the like. I could not deny this "little" sum, 15,000 euros, when I had supported him this far. I had received another salary, from which I could use some part for this expense. I used all the credit on my credit cards to get hold of the sum needed. I also had some shares that I could sell. Had I already paid for his journey and more, I could not refuse to pay for this step on his way home. I just had to sell most of the shares to raise this money. I emptied all small accounts of some hundred or thousand crowns that I had and managed after a day or two to gather as much as was asked for. I was extremely nervous, and I could never sleep without taking sleeping-tablets. I was in a constant state of worries about the money I was expected to send for Edward's expenses, and he stressed me by asking several times a day if the bank had granted the loan, or if I could use another bank than before, if they refused to give another loan. Since I had paid back all my loans some years earlier, my credit trustworthiness was very good. The risk level was estimated to be 0.1% for my creditors. I transferred the money to the same Turkish account holder that had been used earlier for my transactions to the Recess Department and Anderson.

I logged in to my bank account from which the transactions were made once an hour to see if the new money from the sale of shares had arrived with my bank account. I also wanted to know if my transaction to the Turkish bank account had gone through. I checked my cell phone to see if there was a new message from Edward. He tried many times to make a phone call, but I didn't answer when he called. Either I was feeling too upset to be able to talk to him or anyone else, or I was busy working at the college, or it was inconvenient for me to answer for other reasons. He asked me when he could talk to me on the phone, and I suggested a specific time when we could talk. On two occasions, we had short talks, both with a bad sound transmission. On the first occasion, it was on a Saturday in December, I was standing in the railway station of the town I used to visit for my shopping trips. I didn't hear every word he said, but I realized he was worried about something. He said he was okay, not more. I had a feeling something was wrong, but I didn't want him to talk about the problem on the phone. According to the time schedule, he was about to fly home. Just like the month before, I was worried he would cling to me after he got home, or that something else would go wrong. Later that evening I saw an explanation why he had sounded so downhearted.

He sent a picture from his passport, which showed that the date for his passport had expired. The date for expiration was November 27, and now was December 6. The staff at the airport denied him admittance to the plane. They said he was illegally in the UK, since he had no valid document to show he was allowed to visit the UK, no visa. He wrote messages where he sounded extremely disappointed. "I seem to be cursed", he wrote. I was very disappointed too. He had walked to the American Embassy in London and asked them what to do. They had told him there were two options for him, both entailing 1,300–1,500 euros more to pay. Which option would he take? He asked me to give him a new loan to pay for the less expensive option, but it would take some days to get this document, and meanwhile he had to stay at a hotel. To make things worse there was a strike or lockout on the Embassy that would procrastinate the issue of a new document. He said he had watched out for the most inexpensive hotels, but no matter which hotel he would stay at, this would mean a lot of money that he didn't have in cash. I later learned the name of the hotel, and in the advertisements on the Internet they boasted to be an affordable hotel with good service.

I had to find fresh money for these new expenses. Now I had no more accounts to make withdrawals from. I had to ask for a bank loan. I searched Internet and tried asking for loans without phone calls. Since Edward would pay back very soon I didn't have to ask for a long-time loan; the loan would be redeemed within a very short time. I just applied for a three-year-long loan in a Norwegian bank. I submitted my application and was granted the loan within a few minutes. The sooner Edward could return home, the quicker the loan would be redeemed, I reasoned. It took some days before the loan was deposited on my own bank account. I was relieved when the money transaction had been completed, and there was a short period when I didn't have to feel so extremely fidgety as I was before the loan was granted. I told Edward it was done, and he assured me he would pay back with some extra interest for my honesty and patience. "I won't disappoint you", he assured me.

In the intervals between the different loans we had long chats about all kinds of things. He talked about his son and the son's teacher. They were so fond of each other, they had bonded from the very first day in school. "It must be wonderful to know that your son is so well taken care of", I said. I searched the Internet for information about this teacher that Edward had told me about. I didn't find her name on the boarding school for boys that I found in Baltimore. They don't include all teachers' names on the web sites of the schools. You don't find the names of the teachers on a Swedish school's website, unless you are a student or a parent of a student at the school. I also saw that the combination of the teacher's first name and her second name was fairly common in the United States. I had first noticed that her name was exactly the same as the receiver of my first bank transaction to the Recess Department. But that person lived according to the information on my receipt in Columnus in Ohio.

Brian wanted to become a medical doctor, Edward told. I assumed that Brian's rating was good enough for him to be admitted to medical studies. His father seemed worried to hear that the demands were very high. He wanted to relocate to a good European country, he said. Would his son like to move to another country? He wasn't sure about that.

His son loved to be on the beach. They would probably spend some days on the beach over the Christmas holiday. He would send me pictures from his home later. He asked me if I would like to go to a spa over Christmas; he would support me financially, he said. I answered I could not go anywhere for Christmas. I was expected to be at home, cooking and socializing with my relatives. At this point I believed by 90% Edward was an honest man. Who would come up with suggestions like that if he wasn't honest?

Over the Christmas weekend we were to have my son, his girlfriend, and my mother in-law as guests. We would be five persons to eat a lot of good Christmas dishes, and have a nice time together. The house should be decorated with Christmas decorations, there should be electric lights in a Christmas tree outdoors, and Advent stars in the windows. The menu for each day must be planned and a lot of drinks had to be purchased. We had agreed not to buy more than one Christmas gift for each of us. I hoped Ingemar's girlfriend would align with our generally restrictive attitude. I was worried my money wouldn't suffice for all these extra things after the bank loan installments had been paid. I had to reserve some part of my salary for this purpose!

Edward sent a picture of a beautiful Christmas tree, and wished me and my family a merry Christmas. On New Year's Eve, he sent a message wishing a Happy New Year. He said the new year would most likely be fine for me. "I hope you're right", I answered but I felt far from certain it would.

I wondered what Edward was doing all these days at his hotel room, but I dared not ask him. I wanted to keep him at a distance, I must not be sentimental, not pity him and not show my compassion for him in my messages. I rather wanted to be strict, neither harsh to him nor too open with my feelings. I sometimes felt a strong aggression towards him because of all the problems he had caused me. By myself I called him all kinds of nasty words, and I regretted very much having embarked on this terrible roundabout with money, I wanted so eagerly it would soon be over.

EDWARD'S CHILD GETS ILL

I t was obvious that Edward wanted to give his only child a good upbringing, even if he hadn't been able to be around as an everyday parent. Edward talked about his son in a sensitive way. He told me Brian had some health issues, his teacher had told him. He was worried about that. One day Brian had been rushed to hospital. There was some problem with a kidney. I expressed my sympathy for him and his son, and I assured him his son would soon recover from his illness. "Amen", he answered. But the next day he told me that the situation for his son was critical. The doctors needed to make an operation on him, but it was an expensive operation, it would cost 26,000 euros. Being in London without access to his bank account, he couldn't pay for the operation. The teacher had reported on Brian's health status, and she had been crying when telling him. She would gladly have paid everything, had she been in the possession of the means. She had already emptied her account for the legal process that had released Anderson from his custody. The question was now: Could I help him, that is take a bank loan for this purpose? He pleaded to me in a very pathetic way. He said I was his savior, and he was so depressed that he could neither eat nor drink. He would never more bother me with any problem.

I was suffering from severe psychological problems at this time. I had to take sedative medicine to cope with my duties at work and at home. I had attacks of panic every morning. I felt like something terrible was about to happen. I feared I had made a serious mistake when I had entered into this business and I had no one to ask for advice. I had to keep quiet about the whole thing despite my state of mind. I was scared to receive all these messages from Edward where he implored me to lend him more money. I had already lent him much more than I really could afford. I lost my appetite for both food and drink. I just had to pretend everything was as usual. When Christmas was approaching, I had lost about 20 pounds. I was very worried about the coming holidays. How would I cope to be a nice hostess at the same time as Edward sent those messages about money? I came to the conclusion I had to quit from this heavy assignment. I had to turn away from Facebook and stop reading his messages. There was always a message waiting for me every morning.

The next morning, I didn't read the message from Edward, I just wrote a message to him saying that I was ill and could not talk to him any longer. Soon after, I got a message from the Recess Department, which told me that if I wanted their agents to help my friend, I had to act soon. I answered that I was ill and couldn't do anything more. They expressed their sympathy with me and said I should take my medicine to recover. But I was also told that an agent had been in touch with Anderson and he had asked her to urge me to resume the communication with him.

That same day he used email to contact me and his e-letter contained so many sensitive words that I couldn't ignore him more, even if I really wanted to be released. I was entrapped! An extremely stressful period started with a heated dialogue between me and Edward.

"Hello My dearest friend good morning. its me Edward please the idea of you not talking to me is not called for please come online and lets talk like before we both understand each other please [...] Please can you come online on facebook I want to talk with you please please please"

I responded that I might be able to scrape together 4,000 euros the following days. But this amount must include the charge for the agent. I would be salaried the same week.

He thanked me but urged me to raise at least 8,200 euros. The son's teacher would sell some things that would yield almost 4,000 euros. This would altogether make 12,000 euros, which would make half payment of the total cost. He would pay the rest when he arrived home, he said. He wanted me to turn on my cell phone again, to take a phone call from the teacher. I protested I couldn't talk on the phone, since I had so much to do at home, and moreover I didn't want anyone to press me for more money. I also pointed out to him that I was feeling very insecure because of all these money transactions. I promised I would do my utmost to find 4,000 euros more for this purpose.

Edward reminded me I should use the Express service for this transaction. It was urgent to make the operation of his son possible as soon as possible.

I felt extremely nervous and tense these days before Christmas when Edward and I were chatting about this money transaction. It was hard to carry through everything that I had to do to raise all the money that was needed, while I was busy preparing before the great holidays.

Why doesn't "the greatest nation in the world" give their citizens a decent health care, no matter how much money they possess? I found it difficult to believe they would let a young brilliant child die, if it was possible to help him get well. They boast they have the best doctors and the best of almost anything in the U.S., but they don't bestow their services on those who really need it! I knew medical care for everybody was a hot potato in the U.S., especially now that Donald Trump had taken office as president.

I searched Internet to find out if things really were as bad as that. Would not a 12-year-old boy be given the health care he needed in this situation? The only child of an American citizen, a man who had fought for his country for so long! I got hits of different contents. An American doctor purported it was not possible for any hospital to deny a citizen life supporting care. Other persons regretted the non-existent medical care in the United States. I told Edward what I had learnt. He said it differed a lot between different states. He was very desperate in his way of asking me to help him.

It was hard for me to brush aside his worries for his son. They sounded very genuine and highly motivated, I had no problem to understand him in this situation. But I had no money left that I could use to pay for the whole operation and the agent's trip to the U.S., which would cost some 1,200 euros. After some pondering about it I told Edward I would try to scrape together something like 4,500 euros. I had received a new salary since the last time I gave him a loan.

I had to apply for a bank loan, and as quickly as possible. I spent a lot of time searching banks and other credit institutions on Internet. It was surprisingly easy to apply for a loan, so called blanco loans for which there is no property as a warrant for the loan. You fill out a few data about your place of residence, monthly income and some other details. Within a few minutes you get a response from the bank. The banks send a request to a credit-giving agency that gives information about your credit rating. In my case the credit rating was 0,1%, which is very good. I had redeemed all my old bank loans, I had no debts, which was my safety before my retirement. After my retirement, I would have to live on about half the sum I had available while still working. I turned to a Norwegian bank and I was granted a loan of 150,000 at an interest rate that I deemed reasonable. Since I knew I would be able to pay back very soon, I thought I could choose a short time for paying back this loan. I would have three years to pay back this loan. This meant I would have to pay installments of about 600 euros every month! There would however be no problems, since I would be able to pay back very soon. These were my thoughts. Still I was extremely nervous about taking this bank loan. I checked every second hour my bank account into which the loan would be deposited. And Edward asked me many times a day about the loan. He was very impatient to know about the money and if the application for a bank loan had been successful. He was worried I would not be granted a loan.

"I am so worried. Please what is the problem. Did anything go wrong? Please my heart is beating hard"

It took two days before the loan was available and I was able to carry out the transaction. I told Edward I could lend up to 8,000 euros, nearly double the sum I had more or less promised him before. This was a piece of good news for him. And he promised again he would pay back immediately he came home.

"Thanks for your trust. It's rare to find. Thanks so much. I will never disappoint you. Immediately I leave here I will transfer all the money to you. I swear. Don't have any fear of that at all. I have the money just for me to get home."

When I told the Recess Department that Anderson needed more financial support, this time for his son who needed an operation, they asked me if I was pressed to give money. The man or woman who wrote the messages was always anonymous. Only on one occasion, and after my request, did a man give his name. The board wanted to discuss this matter, they wanted me to tell them about the purpose of the transactions. Edward told me later in his text messages that they also had asked him a lot of things: about his hotel, room number, the name of his son's doctor and more. He was very scared he said, because the Recess Department had all his social security in their hands, they knew everything about him. It was a "sensitive department" he said. What he meant by this was not clear. I didn't know how sincere I should be in my answer to the Board of the Recess Department. Should I say anything about my worries and the doubt I had about Anderson's chances to pay back? At this point, I believed Edward would pay back, even though I had some doubts about his character in general. He had sworn three times that he would ask for no more money. I told Edward about the request from the Recess Department to tell them about the situation. I was relieved to hear that he wanted me to tell the truth about everything. I wrote a letter to them where I admitted that the expenses for Anderson had been much larger than I had expected, but that I trusted Mr. Anderson to pay back as soon as he returned home.

My answer seems to have reassured the Board that this was no case of extortion but a friendly loan to him. They praised me in the next letter saying that I was a very good and generous woman. They had checked everything about Mr. Anderson and found that it was "legit", correct. I transferred the money for the son's medical care. I was a prey of conflicting feelings all the time. One day I felt relatively calm that this would end well, the next day I was sweating because of the anxiety that this was possibly a confidence trick played on me. Fortunately, my husband didn't notice my state of mind.

One evening when I was searching Internet to find a reasonably good loan, my husband was talking about loans in general terms and he praised me for having no bank loans. "You are rare in this respect", he said. "Almost everyone has bank loans to pay installments to". It was an absurd situation for me. I was anything but calm about my economic situation. He was laughing while talking about those stupid persons who gave loans to persons they didn't really knew. One case of fraud that was reported in the local newspaper was about a man who had got to know a young attractive woman on a web site for dating. The woman who turned out to be a man in real life just needed some financial help for a special purpose. The man had given a loan, but had later discovered it was a fraud. My husband laughed at the story. "How stupid can you be?", he asked referring to this duped man. Well, how stupid could I be? I am usually not gullible, I am rather suspicious, and I considered myself capable of assessing people's character if I have known them for some time.

The 8,000 euros did not cover everything that the operation on Brian would cost. I don't know how they solved the situation at the hospital, but Anderson told me that Maria and the most senior teacher at the boarding school had visited the manager of the hospital and asked for some days of grace with the payment. Perhaps they had also managed to press the costs for the operation as well. If they couldn't pay the whole sum of money right away, Mr. Anderson would make up for the rest when he had returned home. Edward told me later that his son had been successfully operated on, he had talked to him on the phone. Brian sounded fine.

When the Recess Department wanted me to account for all the expenses I had had for Anderson so far, I told them about the cost for a new passport. The Recess Department said that applying for a special document from the Embassy that Anderson needed for his home return was totally wrong. Anderson would have to go by a special plane for his flight home; it was their task to make it possible for him to go home safely. All this trouble about the document at the Embassy and the extra time it had taken because of the strike had been a waste of time and money! Anderson never told the Embassy that he was a military person, he thought that this might cause more troubles for him. He was probably right.

It was not my idea to apply for this document, it was of course Edward's, which he admitted. The Recess Department would take care of this matter. The problem was they charged a cost of 13,000-15,000 euros for this! I asked them why this flight was so extremely expensive, nearly ten times as high as a normal flight to the U.S. They answered that Anderson needed another type of flight than civil people. This flight meant a safe way without embarrassing interviews at the airport, a safer plane for people who work for the UN. We should "join our hands" to make the flight home for Anderson possible, they told me. "Joined hands" in this case meant my raising more money for this purpose. Neither the officials at the Recess Department nor Anderson seemed to understand what immense trouble it would be for me to raise this money.

A HOTEL WITH WICKED PERSONNEL

Edward complained about the way he was treated by the hotel staff. He said they were rude, even wicked, to him. The reason why they were so unkind to him was most likely the fact that he hadn't paid anything for his stay so far, and he had already stayed there for several weeks. He needed money to pay for the hotel. Edward asked me what "we" would do to pay the hotel bill. "I don't know" I answered, feeling awkward. "OK", he answered. He put all responsibility for his wellbeing on my shoulders. While I wanted most of all to fend him off! I cried when I was alone. Why had I been entrapped like this? I had been too kind and stupid at the same time. I thought anyone would be wiser and cooler than I was in this situation.

Again, I had to search for a way to get a bank loan. I tried to augment the previous bank loan I had taken, but the bank immediately declined my request. I searched among my paper documents from different banks that I had gathered when I was looking for a loan, some weeks earlier. I had wanted to throw all these forms in the trash, but for some vague reason, I had saved them in a drawer in my writing-desk. I felt very stressed again. Everything had to be done so fast. Which bank would grant me a quick loan? Should I try two different banks and accept the bank that dealt with my application first? I couldn't be too peculiar about the interest rate. The speed with which the application was approved was the most important thing for me.

I felt the darkness in December penetrate into my soul. I have never as an adult looked forward to Christmas, and this time least of all. I felt like going away somewhere where there were no media, no cell phones, no humans at all. The only beings I would allow to be with me were my cats. I love animals, they give me more peace than humans do.

The Recess Department sent me a push notice that warned me they would have no agents to send if the money wasn't available for them within a very short time. I told them I had big problems to raise the money. After a few more days, I was granted a new bank loan. I couldn't bother myself about the conditions for the repayment of the bank loan. After all, Edward would pay back as soon as he returned home, wouldn't he? When my thoughts touched upon the possibility he would not pay back, I just felt sick. I had to go to the bathroom more often than I usually do. Everything was getting on my nerves. I couldn't listen to my husband talking about trite things without being irritated, I was heartbroken about bad results from my students, I was often impatient because of delayed trains. The darkness and the hustle around Christmas were more intolerable than ever before.

Edward had tried to persuade the hotel director to give him credit until he got home, but the director had flatly refused. They allowed no guests to leave their rooms before they had paid for their hotel stay. The prices were exceedingly high. Both feeding and lodging was expensive. He said he would try to raise money for the hotel stay by working, but the problem was he had no visa for his stay in London. It would be illegal to hire him. I realized it would be impossible for him to pay the hotel bill, but I could no longer support him. I suggested we would contact the American Embassy in London, or some newspapers. Edward didn't like this idea at all. "The Embassy people don't know me", he said. "But it is their job to help the American citizens abroad", I answered. I tried to call the embassy several times but I just got stuck in the switchboard with no adequate options. I wrote an ordinary letter to the Embassy and posted it, I even filled out a form on Internet directed to the Mayor of London. I explained Mr. Anderson's situation and asked them to assist him in his endeavor to get home. It might not be lawful in the United Kingdom to refuse a person like him to leave the hotel because he had no access to his bank account. I got an e-letter from the American Embassy some months later, when Edward had returned home long ago.

What did the hotel director hope for? Would he eventually call the police to take Edward to custody because of his failing to pay? Why was I the only person to pay for everything? I contacted the Recess Department and asked them to do their best to make a deal for Mr. Anderson. They were reluctant to do so, but I pressed them to make a try. I also contacted the lawyer Geoffrey Nelson and asked him to help Edward. I told him I could not pay for more, and even if I had possessed the money, I would not use it for these expenses. He said he would make a try with the hotel staff.

Later that day Edward wrote a message to me where he told me that neither appeal to the director had been successful. They just refused to let him go if he didn't pay. I asked him how long it would take before they called for the police to get him arrested. "Is that what you wish for me?" he asked and made me feel guilty. I couldn't really understand what the hotel director was planning to do if Edward didn't pay. I had never heard of a situation like this. He had stayed at the same hotel for weeks, and he had earlier asked to suspend payment until he returned to the U.S., but had been refused. What were they going to do with this hotel guest? What are they entitled to do by law? I understood that Edward saw me as a savior, and I had been, though against my will. If I was the only one to save him it was urgent to make him leave as soon as possible, since the hotel bill was adding up with every new day. Each overnight stay there cost more than 200 dollars.

Edward complained about the way he was treated by the hotel staff. I asked Edward for a phone number to the hotel. When I had got it, I called the hotel and talked with a harsh person of the hotel staff. I asked what they demanded to let Mr. Anderson go. He mentioned an amount of nearly 10,000 euros if Anderson would leave the next or the day after the next. I don't remember exactly how long he had been staying at that hotel, but it sounded an awful lot for a modest hotel. I am sure they took advantage of the fact that Anderson was in the U.K. illegally. They had probably realized that he was in a troublesome situation and wanted to squeeze as much money as was possible from this predicament, no matter who paid the bill. The man I talked to seemed a bit more reasonable, when I said I would pay for Mr. Anderson. He even promised they would offer him an extra free meal! A few hours later Edward said that I had done wonder with this phone call. They had been kinder than before and had offered him an extra meal! I told him the only thing that had made them forthcoming was the prospect of getting money. He agreed.

It took some time for me to raise the money needed for Edward's hotel bill, and I forgot to mark with a cross the Express option on the bank transaction, which meant it would take some extra day for the money to arrive with the Recess Department. I had to use up all my credit on two different bank cards, and some fresh money from my December salary to get the money. My heart was very heavy, I had a lump of anguish in my breast, while I was waiting for the money to arrive with my bank account. Edward had asked me to lend him some extra money for taxi cars too. I regretted very much having missed the Express option, even though this option was more expensive.

The lawyer confirmed in a letter he had failed to persuade the hotel director to let Edward leave without paying before, and he urged me to make a last effort to support Edward financially. "If you saw him now you would understand he needs love in his situation", he wrote. His letter was more sentimental than usual and he stressed the problems for Edward if he would be arrested by the police. I had asked him about the Habeas Corpus Act, that protects people from being detained without a court's examination. He answered that the hotel bill had to be paid anyway. If Edward would be taken by the police because he didn't pay the hotel bill, Nelson would not be allowed to represent him at court, he said, since Edward had no valid document to stay in England. "Being an illegal occupant in Britain is a big crime, it's a criminal offence", he wrote. He advised something "is done urgently" to help him. He had found Edward in a very bad shape. "This is not a time to lost hope on him."

HOME FLIGHT AND MORE FINANCIAL PROBLEMS

T his was in the middle of January and I was extremely worried about my financial situation. I had hoped for a final solution of my economic problems for so long a time. I tried to convince myself all this would soon be over, and I was planning what I should do when the debts were paid back. I would feel happier and healthier than ever! I would buy some things for my "bonus-children", the young boys and the girl I took care of as their guardian. I would give money for charitable purposes, I would resume my earlier obligations to make monthly donations to the WWF and other charitable organizations. Perhaps I would invest in a better car than the one I had. It would be marvelous; I would be able to breathe freely, I would stop taking sleeping pills. I told Edward many times I couldn't wait till the day when I was able to pay back my bank loans and strengthen my economy. I said my life was miserable with these expenses. He didn't like my talking in this way. "You make me sad when you talk like that", he said.

He never asked me about my profession, but I had casually mentioned my work, in particular when he was impatient to get a new money transfer. He accused me of ignoring him when I didn't answer him right away. I once used the word *extortion* to describe his way to persuade me into giving him loans. He answered in a very agitated way: "Now I feel very disappointed and shameful. You should know that I am an honest man". Later he asked forgiveness because he had been so harsh to me.

I often asked myself why he, the Recess Department and the lawyer always expected me to pay for his expenses. I told Edward many times that

I was neither his mother nor any other relative, and that he had to take responsibility for his own life. I had helped him in October to be released from his service in Syria, and later I was more or less forced to pay a lot expenses because of his decision to bring the sealed money box from his commander. Where would it end? I just had to make him go home and do the right thing for me as soon as possible.

I managed to get a new bank loan, but there had been some hesitation from the bank before they granted the loan. I had tried to conceal that I no longer was holding a tenure at the university, I was serving as a stand-in for a teacher who had had to leave her job earlier than anyone could foresee. It was humiliating for me to admit I had been telling a lie in my application form. I called the director of the hotel again to assure myself Edward would be permitted to leave if an agent from the Recess Department paid the amount of money we had agreed. This time he was sullener than the previous time, but we made a deal. I told him they had to treat Mr. Anderson kindly.

The Recess Department promised that everything would be arranged for, as soon as Edward (through me and the agent) had paid the bill. They would see to it that he would go with the next U.S. plane for Baltimore. Having met with so many setbacks over Edward's long journey home, I was extremely nervous that there would be another obstacle for him to go home.

When I hadn't heard from him for two days, I wrote to the Recess Department asking them if Anderson had arrived in Baltimore, which they confirmed he had; they gave the exact times for departure and arrival. I feared however there would be some trouble when he got home. If everything had been okay he would most certainly have let me know he was home again. I decided to write an e-letter to him, using the Internet address he had used in London. I felt I just had to remind him of the costs I had had for him.

Hello Edward,

According to the staff at UN you took a flight to Baltimore on Friday and arrived in Baltimore on Saturday at 4.56 Swedish time. I was worried that something might have gone wrong again, before I got this information. I hope you have had time to rest and do some urgent things you need to do after being away for so long a time. You must be exhausted after all this! I am!

I will give you the details about my money transfers to you by showing you the receipts from my bank. I have taken three bank loans of 150 000 crowns each. I am anxious to redeem these bank loans as soon as possible. The interest rate varies from 6 to 10%, because I was so stressful when I asked for the loans, that I couldn't wait for the best offer, and I thought it would not be long before the loans could be redeemed. The total sum of the interest rates for these three loans is approximately 300€ if I can pay back this week or next.

You have assured me repeatedly that I can trust you, and for most of the time I have trusted you. But there have been some very critical points when I doubted. I didn't want to jeopardize the little safety I had managed to scrape together, I really don't want to fall into financial misery. I must have means to cope with unforeseen expenses.

You must keep in mind that I have never met you in real life, and the few people I have talked with about this have all been pretty sure that you have swindled me. I have protested against their suspicions, but it has been terrible just to consider that they might be right. I know you will do the right thing and pay back what you owe me. You promised you would deal with this as soon as possible. It will be a great relief for me when loans are away, when my economy is restored again. Please help me to do so.

My best wishes for you and your son

Later that day I had an ordinary phone call, not Messenger call, from Edward, but he was so hoarse that it was almost impossible to hear what he said. I had to go outdoors to answer the call, to prevent my husband from hearing that I was talking on the phone.

I have sometimes problems to catch all the words on the phone, I'm always afraid to misunderstand what the other person at the other end of the communication is saying. That applies also to Swedish, my mother tongue. There is always the risk I give a totally wrong answer. I was worried he would talk about new problems he had, and this time I found it more difficult than earlier to understand what he said, because his voice was husky. I thought he said "I have lost my boy" and that made me very upset. Had his son subdued to his illness? I had to ask him if I had understood what he said correctly. "No, I said I have lost my voice", he said. I felt embarrassed, and at the same time relieved! He had caught a cold which made his voice hoarse. I asked him to *write* a message to me, because I couldn't hear every word he said. Yet I could hear in his way of talking that something was terribly wrong. He said something about *chaos,* but I wasn't prepared to have a deep talk about his problems on the phone. He said that he was currently with the son's teacher. They appreciated what I had done for him and the son. I asked him if he had read the letter I had sent to his email address. He hadn't. He had probably only used a temporary email address while he was staying in London.

But he would go to the bank immediately and transfer the money he owed me. He had all the information about my bank account saved in a book.

PROBLEMS TO RAISE MONEY

M y hopes to regain the money I had lent to Edward were thwarted yet once more. He told me he could not pay back, because the IRS had sealed his property and he had no access to his bank accounts because he had failed to pay taxes, almost 50,000 dollars for house, car and job the last two years. I realized what this meant for me –he would not be able to pay back money to me, as he had promised, even sworn, many times, he would. I would stay put in the deep debt hole for a long time ahead. I felt desperate. I would have to pay about 15,000 crowns in installments to the banks every month, that is more than 60% of my salary after taxes have been deducted. This meant I would go bankrupt sooner or later.

Sometimes I wished I had a gun, like most Americans reportedly have. I felt like committing suicide. Going through this financial hassle would be a painful and humiliating process, the economic position of independence that I had achieved would be lost forever. My husband has a small pension to live on, it is not large enough to support two people and to pay for all the repairs that a house needs. We would be as poor as we were once we were young. I would have to save and scrape for the rest of my life. We would never be able to afford a journey abroad once a year as before.

Edward was begging for money every time he sent me a message. He said, he hoped to live peacefully with his son in their own house. (So he had a house after all? Geoffrey Nelson had told me he only had a rented apartment.) His son should not have to live with his teacher all the time, he said. I told him there was no chance for me to take a loan of 50,000 euros, no bank would give me a loan now that I already had so many loans and credit debts. The loans were blanco loans, i.e. no safety for the loan, but all credit institutes take information from the UC, (*Upplysningscentralen)*, the Information Centre that gives information about a borrower's financial soundness. "How much can you borrow then?" he asked. "Perhaps 15,000 euros" I answered. Edward said it was too small a sum, not even half his tax debts. When he had paid his debts to IRS he would have access to his bank account. He implored me to try my best to raise an amount of 24,000 euros. There were many *please* in his messages.

There must be other ways to solve this problem, I thought. I told him he should ask some economist for advice in this situation. He said he had, but they only advised him to pay back the money he owed the IRS. Some advice!

I was aware there had been warnings that I had ignored. The lawyer had told me that Anderson had no property of his own in the U.S.; Nelson had also told me that Anderson had bills that should have been paid a long time ago. Edward never boasted being rich, but by letting me see his bank account of almost 400,000 dollars, he had made me believe he had a solid economy, solid enough to pay back what he owed me and the son's teacher. Edward had said "I am not poor". I interpreted this as equivalent of "I have a modest income", and guessed he meant he wasn't a millionaire –in dollars. 400,000 dollars are converted into Swedish crowns equal to more than three million crowns. Some decades ago, being a millionaire meant being very rich. Today you should own much more than just a few million crowns, to be considered wealthy. By American standards I suppose this amount is even more modest, since Americans do not have the social benefits they have in most Western countries. I had reacted against the high cost for Anderson junior's operation.

I wondered how Edward had been able to withhold so much money from the IRS (The Internal Revenue Service). For most citizens, it is considered a sacred duty to pay taxes, and usually this is no matter of honesty. Whether you are employed by a private corporation or a state institution, a certain percentage of your salary will be deducted from your salary by your employer. Taxes in Sweden are relatively high, among the highest worldwide, but then we have a much larger sector of social welfare than in the U.S., including hospitals, care centers, education. Our society is less characterized by segregation than the American; the living conditions are better for families with low incomes than in most other countries. Only in large cities like Stockholm and Gothenburg, the differences in life styles between different socio-economic groups are noticeable.

I had told Edward that it was impossible for me to raise those amounts of money he wanted, since I have no fortune, I just had enough money to cope with some extra expenses like re-equipment of machinery in my house. He said "ok" but he didn't seem to understand or accept that answer. He once asked me what kind of car I had, and he was hardly impressed by the answer that I had a Nissan car. Foreigners usually connect Sweden with Volvo cars. Volvo stands for both quality and quantity; you need a lot of money to buy a new Volvo car, but most people purchase a Volvo by installments.

When Edward continued to ask for help to pay his back taxes I was alarmed. Would it never end – this lending roundabout? Would this loan be the final step that led to unsealing his bank account and paying back the money he had borrowed from me? Edward dismissed or just ignored my proposals for him to collect money. I asked him if he could show me a letter from the IRS saying that they would unseal his bank account if a certain part of the back taxes were paid. He answered it was not possible. I tried to be adamant in my refusal to give more loans. On one occasion, I said "Enough is enough!" and he answered "it sounds as if we were fighting but we are mature persons, parents, and we understand each other well, don't fight me, help me please please please."

I wanted Edward to try other ways to raise money than use me as his emergency bank. I suggested he should start a crowd funding on Facebook, which I know to be a way to gather money from friends or other sympathizing people. Edward answered that I was the only friend on his FB account, and he doubted there existed anyone else who would be so kind to help him. "You have managed to make me very generous, though we don't know each other well", I said. He didn't comment on my somewhat sarcastic remark.

The son's teacher had taken a loan on her house to help him in his troublesome situation, Edward said. And he would himself sell valuable things he had to collect more money. He later told me he had sold everything, even clothes and kitchen equipment to raise money. But he was short of just a few thousand dollars. Could I help him with that little money? He needed about 7,000 euros for the loan and some 2,500 euros for transportation and some other things, all in all 9,500 euros. I answered it would be extremely difficult for me, since I already had four bank loans for his sake, and two heavily used bank credit cards. I would have to use the small amount that was left on my salary bank account, but that would still not be enough for him.

There are however some credit institutes that grant you smaller amounts of money with a high interest rate. That would be the only choice for me. I finally bowed to his insistent pleas and applied for a new loan. My heart was pounding hard when I took a fifth bank loan. Some week later I transferred a lesser sum to him from my salary plus some money from credit cards. These loans were the ninth and the tenth loans to Edward!

I couldn't walk on thinner ice! Edward had called me a savior, but this business would also need a salvation of the savior. I kept telling myself that Edward probably was an honest man. He was after all an officer, and all military personnel have to give an oath that they will be decent in their behavior. The *soldier's creed* says among other things that "No matter what the situation I am in, I will never do anything, for pleasure, profit, or personal safety, which will disgrace my uniform, my unit or my country". To deceive a woman of all her life savings in order to be released from your service, should be considered to disgrace the soldier's uniform, unit and country.

My feelings towards Edward were a roller-coaster between strong hatred and some compassion for him and trust in him. In my thoughts, all the different moments of our communication were turning around. I didn't know for sure which version of Edward was the most trustworthy one. I tended more and more to feel anger and disgust and I felt I had to do something about it. He would not get away with this evil deed against me, no matter if he was "just" a careless liar, not a common swindler.

MARIA MACMILLAN – THE DEVOTED TEACHER

I wondered why Brian's teacher was willing to help Brian's father in his predicament. It became more understandable as I later heard that she was very committed to her work and that she really loved Brian. I suppose it is easier to bond with the pupils in a boarding school than it usually is in a day school. Ms. MacMillan was Brian's mentor. Edward wrote quite a few messages about Brian and his school. I realized that, if Brian was very worried, then the teacher wanted to relieve him from his anxiety. Brian was probably more close to his teacher than to his father emotionally. She contributed with 24,000 euros for the legal process in London; that was her life savings, he told me. But she had complained that she really wanted them back soon, because her house needed repairing.

Brian was more mature than his class-mates were, Edward said. I got the impression Brian was a bit lonesome. I felt sorry for him, his mother being dead and a father who for the most time was absent. I guessed the relationship between Brian and his father was not a very good one. Edward had earlier told me that he was a bit worried how he would cope to live together with a young boy, his son.

At this time, while Edward and I were fighting over money he needed in order to pay his back taxes, I was contacted by Maria MacMillan, Brian's teacher, via email. Maria emphasized in her letter that she had decided to write to me without Edward knowing it. Brian, his son, had given her my email address. Edward had refused to give her my telephone number, saying that he had to get my permission before giving it.

She wanted me to respond urgently and so I did. In my letter to her I described my situation as strenuous because of Edward's constant asking for more and more money. I told her my husband didn't know anything and would be furious if I told him about the loans. I told her that I might be forced to change my telephone number and close my Facebook account, because I was so depressed.

The last but second time Maria wrote to me, she addressed me with the formal *Madam*. She reported she had been to the IRS office and learnt that half the tax debts had been paid, but she probably didn't know this had been made possible thanks to my bank loans. She said that I had got the whole thing about Edward all wrong. She described him as an honest man who tried all means to pay back to me. She had lent money to him earlier, and would also lend him money in this situation. She would help him since she knew his son was very worried that his father would lose everything. If Edward would be able to pay his debts to the IRS she was 100% sure that they would unseal the blocked bank account. Then he would be able to pay back to me what he owed me. At the end she implied that times in the U.S. had become hard because of the new turn of politics. Edward was not to be blamed for this situation. If we joined hands to help him "back to life" again, he would never forget that, she wrote.

I tried to explain what my situation was like. I told her that I had already given Edward large loans, and I told her of the warnings about fraud in this situation.

> I have read what you wrote to me. You know Edward personally, I don't. You don't understand what I have been through these last three months. My husband often asks me "What are you brooding on?" and I can't tell him, because he would be furious if he knew. Three persons have each warned me not to believe in a person I have never met, and they have even told me to go to the police.

> Brian is lucky to have such a devoted teacher as you. And Edward is lucky to have a friend like you. I believe I have contributed to his happiness as much as I can do.

Maria sent a short answer urging me to raise as much money as I could. I would tell her how much I could raise. She would try to help him to complete the balance. She wanted him to pay back to both her and me.

I observed the same tendency to write in a very colloquial way, as the lawyer Geoffrey Nelson had done. She used contracted forms of words, but sometimes she used homophonic words instead of the correct word forms: *his* for *he's*, *its* for *it's* and *loose* for *lose*.

Maria's letters contributed to my feelings of responsibility for Edward's life, and to feelings of guilt that I didn't offer Edward more loans. I felt I just had to do something more to bring this errand to a definite end. I searched desperately Internet for another bank loan, and after some hesitation from the bank I had got another loan of 24,000 euros. This was the tenth time I gave him a loan. I was now deeply indebted, my pulse was high, I sweated profusely and I trembled when I thought of all the debts and the misery they would lead to. The Recess Department sent an agent with the 26,000 euros (I had managed to scrape together another 2000 euros from my bank account). I hoped the IRS would lift their block from Edward's bank account if he paid half the debts. Edward sent a snapshot of a letter he had received from the IRS. It was signed by an official at the local office of the IRS. She informed Mr. Anderson that the remaining balance payment of 28,430 dollars must be paid on or before February 10. When the payment had been received, they would inform the bank so as to unseal the account and his property.

There were a few relatively happy days when Edward seemed to be pretty at ease with his situation. He said he would love to see me some day. He asked me why I had helped him considering the universal problems with scam. I answered that I was happy to have been able to help him, a stranger to me, but it had taken a heavy toll on my mind. I had told the officials at the credit institutions that he was probably an exception to the rule that those who ask for financial help this way are scammers. An official told me that they often simulate that they are in a precarious situation where they need help. But Edward would pay back, I believed. I should not however say *Thank you* to him, before I saw the money deposited on my bank account.

After my last transfer of money, I expected Edward to be able to pay back to me. But I received no money the next days, and Edward told me that there were some restrictions on his bank account, he couldn't use it for a transaction abroad like this.

To strengthen Edward's case towards the IRS, I wrote a letter to the tax official who had sent a letter to Edward, where she confirmed that a part of his tax debts had been paid. Edward had sent a photo of this letter, most likely to assure me he used my money for the right purpose. There was no email address to her in the letter, but after searching Internet I found the official's name on a web site for the IRS. I wrote a letter to her pleading for Edward, emphasizing that he had a 12-year-old son, i.e. a child. I referred to the Convention on the Rights of the Child, that has been laid down as a law, and has been signed and ratified by almost all the countries that are members of UN. The United States is the only state that has signed, but not ratified this Convention. The convention is considered to be important to protect the rights of children. I referred to the contents of this convention, to convince her that the IRS would unseal the bank account for Mr. Anderson. I gave an account of my own relationship to Anderson, telling her that being Anderson's friend I had financially supported his journey home, and that I even had paid a large part of the back taxes.

I received no response from the official that had signed the letter from the IRS. I looked for another person to direct my appeal to, working in the same department as she. When I found a workable name at the same department, I wrote an e-letter referring to the letter I had previously written to her colleague, hoping this would make her feel obliged to respond to me.

Two months later I received a response from the IRS, this time by the ordinary post, which forced me to tell my husband about the whole thing.

EDWARD PAYS BACK?

S ince Edward had no access to his bank account he could not transfer money to me. Edward told me however he would use another bank account, that had belonged to his late father, to pay back what he had borrowed, the major part at least. He had the right to make withdrawals from this bank account, since he was "next of kin". He sent a snapshot of the bank form he had filled in, with all the necessary information about the receiver. The name of the account holder was a man with a surname, typical of German language, indicating his father had another surname than his son. Why had he changed his surname? Had his father's German surname been an impediment in his military career? He didn't comment on the name, and I felt so immensely grateful that the economic problems I had, would soon be eliminated, that I didn't bother him about it. He had sent 100,000 dollars to me, I could see he had paid a transfer cost of 17 dollars, and the money would arrive with the receiver within three days. I just answered "Oh, thanks!" I was so immensely happy that I had not been mistaken about his honest character. At last my loans to him had been repaid. Not altogether, but Edward said he would send the rest on a later occasion. It didn't matter if I didn't get back every dollar I had sacrificed. I had had to economize the last months, since the loans had become due for payment. Now I felt rich, even though I would have less money than before I got to know Edward. I would of course redeem the loans and bank credits first of all. Then I would give some money to charitable organizations as I had done before this happened. I would be able to buy some things for the children whose guardian I was. But above all, I was so happy that I had been right in my assessment of Edward's character. He was one of the exceptions to all the scammers on Internet. There do exist some honest people who use social media to ask for help! This merry-go-round with money transfers would eventually end. It would not be known to my husband. We could go on living in safety knowing that the little money we had saved would be used for the things we needed most.

I was going to write a long thank you letter to him when I had received the money, now that I had the definitive proof that Edward was an honest man. But I couldn't be completely sure before the money had arrived with my bank account. There had been so many setbacks with Edward. Either he was an extremely unlucky man, or he was very successful at tricking me.

The following days I logged into my bank account several times to check if the money had arrived. It hadn't after three days, and I told Edward I had got no money. He said he would visit the bank to hear what was wrong and then call back to me. Some hours later he told me that the money had been "hanging in the air", because there must be a certain percentage of the amount on the bank account for the transaction to go through. He would have to make a deposit amounting to 18,000 dollars to receive a reflection pin he said. He wanted me to send as much money as possible to him the next days. It was however impossible for me to lend him anything at all. I was now using my credit card to pay for food, and all the necessary things we needed for everyday life. All my bank accounts had been emptied.

So much for my hopes to put this terrible terror I had lived through the last three months to an end! I told Edward many times that I was not able to lend him one single dollar more, he had emptied all my pockets. The ball was with him. He had to pay his debt to me. I was in a desperate need for money myself.

Every time he talked to me, he asked me if I could help him "with the little that remained" for him to pay for a reflection pin. He returned many times with the same appeal: "Can you somehow raise 3,000€ for me?" He even suggested I should buy some things with my credit cards to send to him, and he would sell them in order to collect the money needed. I either answered with a clean NO or didn't answer at all. But he wouldn't take no for an answer. He said I could ask my husband or friends to lend money. He acted as if he didn't remember what I had told him very clearly earlier: I have no wealthy husband nor friends, and I would never ever ask them for a loan. My financial independence is very dear to me, a sacred thing.

In March I was close to a mental breakdown because of the mounting anxiety within me. Edward's messages to me were sporadic appeals to just give him a little more help. Every day was an Inferno for me. The first thing I felt when I woke up after a night's sleep was the immense fear I had for the inevitable economic disaster. The fear that my family would suffer because of me, and the dreadful feelings of guilt that I had, tore on me. I was totally mistaken in the surmise that Edward would be the only honest man who used social media to collect money. I had not trusted those many warning lamps I had seen. I had had a romantic idea that an officer of the American army would be more scrupulous than Edward had been.

MY HUSBAND LEARNS
ABOUT THE LOANS

On March 13 when my husband had picked up the post, he said there was a letter to me from the IRS, (the Internal Revenue Service) in the U.S. He said I should hand over the letter to him, since he is much more familiar with the contents of such a letter than I am. He worked earlier as a tax lawyer at the Swedish tax office. I was alarmed when I saw the letter and realized that I would have to tell him everything about Anderson and the debts I had incurred because of him. I will remember this day forever as a very dark day of my life. I just couldn't construe an explanation other than the truth. The time of secretive searching for bank loans, the constant demands from Edward to pay more and more had to be finished! This was the moment I had feared most the last five months. I had hoped all this would be over before my husband knew anything about it. He would never have known anything at all about these loans, if Edward had paid back as he had promised to do.

My throat felt like tied up, but after a minute I said "I have something to tell you." I told him the most important parts of the story that were pertinent to the bank loans. My husband is not a good listener, he stopped me when I had revealed the sums of bank loans, and was just furious. He wasn't interested in hearing about my emotional ups and downs in the course of this story. His view was clear: I was stupid to believe such a man. He never believed I would be so stupid. Didn't I realize that everything this racketeer had told me were fake stories? I was petrified with fear when I heard him, it was impossible to go on telling about the turns this story had taken and make his view more balanced. And I feared he was right in his opinion. I told him I had had plans to commit suicide, to get away from this catastrophe, and to make amendments to the economy. The assurance company would pay out some money if I died. It would not however be more than a very modest amount of money.

I did my best to assure my husband he was wrong about the identity and the character of the persons involved in the story. He believed that the son's teacher and other persons involved in this story, were one and the same person, who just played different roles in his communication with me. I wrote an e-letter to Maria MacMillan asking her to say something about her true intentions. I told her that my husband had been told about the loans to Edward and was very angry with me. Maria never responded to my call for help. Yet I believe that she was a friend of Anderson and his son's teacher, not the same person as him.

Sven, my husband, demanded I give him the agreement forms related to the bank loans immediately. He was obviously very disappointed with me. I had helped a man who was almost a stranger to me. I thought I did something good, at least in the beginning of our acquaintance. And I had believed my loans to him would be paid back in a near future. Now it felt like I was an embezzler, even though I had used my own money; I had taken personal loans. But I was guilty of doing something secretly without my husband knowing about it. He would never ever have accepted these "loans" to a stranger and he would never even have opened an account on Facebook. He is very critical of social media. He is a decent man who is kind to people he knows well, but he would never have embarked on a business like the one I had done. He tends to divide people into two categories: Those who are okay, even good, and those who are not. He is not interested in psychological issues, he doesn't like talking about relationships, and he is not a man who digs into the minds of other people.

I was very grateful that he helped me to solve the imminent economic problems. I could not confide to him the different ways I had been persuaded to take these loans, he wasn't interested in hearing my emotional turmoil over the time this friendship had lasted. For him the whole thing was above all a big practical and financial issue. Anderson was in his opinion a common swindler who had succeeded in taking me in. "They know how to ingratiate themselves with people, especially weak people" he said. I was characterized as a weak person, one that is easily deceived, not to say stupid. Well, I had been too generous to someone who probably didn't deserve the sacrifices I had made. It is not fair to characterize me as a weak individual though. I am certainly a soft and sensitive person, but usually not weak. I am not good at arguing with people who are aggressive to me. I was for some years bullied by schoolmates in high school. Most people are weak on some spots and on some occasions in life.

In the letter from the IRS, an official just stated that I had neither indicated Anderson's Social Security Number, nor had I been authorized by Anderson to act on his behalf. There was nothing they could do to help me or the person concerned in my letter.

I showed the passport photo that Edward had sent when he was on the airport in London. "How do you know that he is that man on the passport" my husband asked. "Ask the American Embassy if the person on that passport photo is an American citizen!" I mailed the Embassy in Stockholm enclosing this photo. They answered quickly, "The photo has been clearly altered. You should contact your local police". I was very upset when I heard this. Was this conclusive evidence that Edward was a fraudster?

Eric wanted me to write a message to Anderson where he would speak his voice. I translated his words into English and wrote a message to Edward: "I'm Lisa's husband and I've heard about your lies to her. You will not get away with this. We will take judicial proceedings against you."

Edward answered immediately: "No, my friend. I cannot lie. I owe your wife a lot. With some help, she will have her money back within two days."

"We have shown your passport photo to the American Embassy in Stockholm. They said it had clearly been altered".

"Who? Why? Do you guys want to make troubles? Don't threaten me."

"You made her believe that you have money on a bank account large enough to pay back. Fake stories."

Edward: "She saw the bank account herself!"

Sven was not in the mood to go on with this conversation. Edward tried to call me on Messenger, but I didn't answer. I was way too upset to talk to him.

The following days we were both in a very bad mood. My husband ranted about my bank loans, asked me to give him all the agreements with interest rates and conditions for the bank loans. This would be very devastating for our economy, he said.

"You will never get anything back from that man! He will never do the right thing. And you have done all this behind my back! We will be poor pensioners. We won't be able to do anything to improve our living conditions, we won't be able to pay for repairs or re-equipment when machines go to pieces".

The following day Edward sent a message saying he was angry with my husband. I told him what Sven had said about his not paying back to me. "Then prove to him he is wrong. Lend me 3,000 euros more and I can get a reflection pin". I didn't bother to give him an answer. I had told him so many times this was impossible. I was completely out of cash.

There were many days and nights to follow when I just felt deep sorrow, I was so disappointed with Edward, and I despaired of my chances to get anything at all back. My husband became, as time went by, more resilient to me, and made some additional efforts to alleviate our financial situation. He is good at managing bank accounts, but he is not a good psychologist.

Sven decided to appeal for a new loan on our house and property. Before he handed in his loan application, he made withdrawals from his own bank savings to give me money to pay back the most disadvantageous short credits. This would give us better chances to be granted a bank loan with our property as security. The bank officials scrutinize the total financial situation of the loan taker.

When he visited his bank, they asked him if he had connections abroad that they should be informed about. This was because his wife, I, had taken so many loans, and had transferred so high amounts of money to bank accounts abroad. It's their duty to ask what purposes the money transactions are used to, but he felt these questions about my transactions were very embarrassing.

We lived a simple life the following months, with no excesses, no journeys, no superfluous things at all. I had cancelled all plans to do something that would involve money spending. My husband seemed to enjoy life almost as usual. In summer, he is busy doing a lot of outdoor activities like chopping wood, planting trees, mowing the lawns we have on our property. He loves nature, spending time in the forest makes him feel happy.

I felt depressed and I couldn't help missing all the things that I would have done if this hadn't happened to me. I spent a lot of time on Internet searching information that could be useful for me. I visited websites for the UN Police, police authorities and the Defense Department in the U.S. The Defense Department was probably accountable for the expenses concerning their military personnel. I tried desperately to request economic compensation for my expenses on Anderson's journey home. I directed my letter to the Defense Minister of the U.S. – Jim Mattis. In the letter, I gave the outlines of the story about Anderson and attached files containing the receipts for all the bank transmissions I had made.

After a few weeks, I got mail from the Defense Department, where they refused to acknowledge there even was a Recess Department. Their staff had full access to their bank accounts, they said. This acquaintance with Anderson was scam, someone had impersonated a member of the Army to deceive me of money.

Dear Ms.

––––––––

This is a scam. The individual that contacted you who claims to be ███████████ is impersonating a member of the U.S. Army. He is not an actual member of the U.S. military.

The ███████████ does not exist within the DoD and neither do the agents that required all those "fees." The application for leave/Vacation that you completed is a false document. There is no such document as a leave form that spouses, fiancés, girlfriends, etc. need to complete. The process for requesting leave is only between the service member and their commanding supervisor. There is also no fee or charge for requesting leave. And we do not charge our military members for flying back home when their leave is approved. The U.S. government provides transportation at the government's expense.

Service members have access to their own personal financial accounts. The DoD does not prohibit their employees from having their own personal accounts.

Scammers use actual photos of service members that they find on-line and create fake profiles and accounts on social media sites in order to create relationships. They use public computers which make it difficult to track these criminals. They also can easily falsify documents by copying and pasting our logos from off the internet. Detailed information about their methodologies and helpful tips to know if you are being scammed can be found by visiting the U.S. Army Criminal Investigation Command website for Reporting A Crime. - - -

This was concrete information about scammers, and they claimed that Anderson and all other persons involved in this case were fraudsters. I understood the word *impersonation* as somebody using a real soldier's name to deceive people in some way. Edward Anderson probably existed as a soldier or had done so, but the man who had been in touch with me on Facebook was not him! The department denied the existence of a department that I had been in close contact with several times. It was difficult to accept their answer as the whole truth.

I doubt the Defense Department was open about this errand. There are activities within the Department that most likely are denied to exist officially. I remembered that Edward had been upset, when I had suggested I write a letter to the Army about the sealed box he brought from his commander. My idea was that the Army would interfere and help Edward be released from custody. "Do you want me to get into still worse problems?" he had answered. "This is a secret way to get a leave from your service in the Army". I found some useful information about fraud on the U.S. Army's website.

Or was the Recess Department an assumed name for a scam network outside of the official military organization? My husband never believed that Recess Department was a legal and trustworthy corporation. In his opinion they are most likely a few shady men who just feign the connection with the U.S. Army and other institutions.

If Recess Department didn't belong to the Defense Department, what other corporation or institution was it part of? Was it a fake department after all? Was this the conclusive proof I had been the victim of a scamming network, not one specific scammer?

MENTAL BREAKDOWN

I am not a cool person who takes troubles easily, in particular not severe economic problems. When I realized that Edward would probably not pay back what he owed me, I entered a state of permanent anxiety. I felt like I was standing on the brink of an abyss. I needed to talk with somebody about my situation as soon as possible. I called the reception of my care center and was given an appointment to the psychiatric clinic. I had a talk with a psychiatric doctor, told her about my situation, and she seemed to understand me well; she advised me to stay at the clinic for a few days to try out an appropriate medicine and therapy. I was not prepared to stay away from my home and my work, but I just couldn't do more. I was living on my nerves; I could not focus on anything. I wanted to get away from this troublesome life. I often thought of a way to kill myself. But what would happen to my husband and my son, if I did so? I should not leave them with a feeling of guilt. I didn't want them to suffer because of my imprudence. I wanted, if possible, to spare them my financial troubles. I would write a letter to my son and explain to him why I had to commit suicide.

I was admitted to a ward with patients with similar symptoms, silent suffering. Some of them were very quiet, didn't ever say a word, some of them had friendly relations to other patients and were talking on this and that. I belonged to those who didn't want to talk at all. I felt very much ashamed of my situation, my illness. Mental illness has always been a kind of stigma in our society. For most part of the time I was just sitting in my room crying or brooding on my situation. I was worried I would not be able to handle my work. I didn't want this terrible situation to interfere with my work. I was stressed by the fact that my work would be delayed, I had to communicate via Internet with colleagues and students without revealing where I was and why. The psychiatrist on the ward talked with me and gave me some new perspectives on my situation and the causes behind my actions. I felt I had to explain why I had got into this situation.

"I am a sensible woman. I usually think over things twice before I do something that entails responsibility or money spending. I have had to be economical to make both ends meet, and to have something saved for rainy days in my life. I don't spend money on gambling or lottery tickets, if it's not for charitable organizations. I was not born with a silver spoon in my mouth, but I have always had money enough to get by. I have been careful not to go beyond the economic frames I have. But for some reasons I can't explain for myself, I spent all the money I had saved for unforeseen expenses, and much much more over five consecutive months for someone I barely knew and for something I should have dismissed as an unreasonable purpose. I regret very much that I was foolish enough to trust a person I never had seen in real life. But I did, at least I did so most of the time I was in touch with him. I thought that I was doing something good for a man who really needed help, a man who was lonely and really needed someone to talk to. Like most other people I enjoy helping people who are in distress for some reason. It is a kick for my self-esteem to know that I have done something that was useful for someone else, whether it is a close friend, a neighbor, family members, or a stranger who is in a difficult situation."

"The important thing is what you feel when you do something, that you consider it to be good for your fellows. It's the intention you have when you start doing something that is most important, not the result of your doings", the doctor said.

"It is the result that is most important", I protested. If you do something that ruins your life or affects the lives of other people in a bad way, you will rightly feel guilt, and you will always regret what you have done."

"When you are entrapped in a situation like the one you have been in, you don't know what it will lead to. The most sensible thing to do for you in this special situation is to relieve yourself of the anxiety you feel; you think you will feel better if you do this. In hindsight, you might find that you made a mistake by doing so. We never know where our decisions will lead us to before we have seen the consequences."

This perspective on the whole thing –I had had a good intention towards someone else– sounded so strange to me after the hard comments from my husband and the terrible remorse I had had. I might have been credulous, but at the same time I had acted in order to help someone.

I stayed at a psychiatric ward because of my great anxiety and depression another two times over the next four months. I was given medicines to cope with the strong feelings I suffered from, and to cope with my sleeping difficulties. I had a few dialogues with a doctor. He tried to make me understand why I had got into this "crisis reaction".

"Have you ever done anything that you knew from the beginning was wrong to do?" he asked. I couldn't remember having done so, apart from very banal things like eating too much, eating the "wrong" things, smoking now and then when I was young.

"You have helped someone, no matter if it is an honest man or not, and that is a good thing. But he has abused this good intention. Would you blame your son if he had given his friend a valuable thing?" he asked.

"I wouldn't, but in this case, it is so much more than just one valuable thing."

"It's the principle of giving, I'm referring to", the doctor said.

"I wouldn't have lent money to him, if I hadn't believed he would pay back. I thought he was honest, but he wasn't. I will have to forgive myself for being so foolish. I can't help thinking this was very wrong", I said.

"In hindsight you know if you have done wrong, but at the moment when you decide to help by giving a lot of money, you don't. It might have been a man who really needed your help very much, we don't know, and then you have done something good. And he could have paid back."

I found the doctor's word soothing, even though I was worried I would not be able to pay the debts caused by these generous loans. After having taken the prescribed medicine, I felt for most of the time a bit better, I had fewer panic attacks. But I was far from well, sometimes I felt waves of sweat through my body in combination with dizziness. Sometimes I was feeling very cold. I couldn't think clearly during the time it lasted. I didn't really hear what other people said, when I felt like this.

After a few days, I was discharged from the hospital, and I resumed my duties as if nothing at all had happened. I am an experienced lecturer, and was able to perform my classes in about the same way I had done so many times before. I forgot temporarily my problems with money and Edward, while I was busy doing my work. Sometimes I got messages from him while working. "Why are you ignoring me?" he asked. I told him the truth that I had other things to do than just serve him.

My professional work as a teacher at the university was not severely disturbed by my troubles with Edward, since I had so many years' practice behind me. But there were other assignments that I had to give up because of my mental problems. I could no longer work as a trustee for a woman that I had taken care of. I hate to leave assignments unaccomplished, but I just felt I couldn't go on with this as before. A doctor I visited urged me to resign from this assignment immediately. "You are in a middle of a crisis, you can't undertake this job too. You have to take care of yourself now", she said. She was absolutely right.

During my stay at the psychiatric ward I had temporarily turned off my Facebook account; it was closed for 14 days. When I reopened it after a fortnight, I soon got a new message from Edward who wondered where I had been. He had tried many times to get in touch with me. He wanted me of course to help him with "the little" that stopped him from sending the money to me. Maybe I had done so, if I had had the means to do so; my capacity to make a sound judgement about this business was gone. I was stony broke, and I didn't know how to cope with my installments that were due at the end of the month. I told Edward that I was being pressed from two men – my husband who ranted about mortgages and Edward who ranted about money to pay for a reflection pin. If I wasn't so sad I would laugh at the situation. "I am sorry about that", he said and I didn't hear from him for a long time.

The second time I was in hospital, a few months ahead, I felt again like I had to finish my life. There was no other solution to my problems. Yet, I contacted the psychiatric clinic and was admitted to their ward as a patient again. My doctor prescribed another medicine to make me feel better and some other pills to take when I needed strongly to calm down. This medicine had a good effect on me immediately. My diagnosis was changed from "Crisis reaction" to "depression". After the discharge from the psychiatric clinic they advised me to have supportive talks with a nurse who was specialized in psychiatrics. I was grateful for this therapy, because I had no one else to talk to about my feelings of guilt and shame.

I had feelings of guilt because I thought I had destroyed not only my own economy, but also the family economy. My salary is badly needed for the maintenance of the house and everything else, and my savings will be needed as the house and machinery wear down year by year. With the bank loans I had taken, we would not be able to pay for repairs or renovations on the house. I was ashamed for letting me be fooled for so long. I am a well-educated woman; I should have known better!

I have been depressed more than once in my life, but this was taking me to even darker places in my mind. I sometimes felt I had to avenge myself on Edward. He would not get away with this cheating. I hated him! By myself I often used all the worst words I know to describe this dishonest man. I remember Edward saying that he would commit suicide, if he couldn't pay back what he owed me. That had sounded so serious! I now realized he had used so strong words to convince me he was a decent man who would keep his promise.

My social life shrank enormously to the absolute minimum level. I rejected meetings with my friends because I felt like crying all the time. I couldn't listen to other people talking, my thoughts were always somewhere else and I didn't want to have guests in my home when I felt like this. At the end of the summer we did have guests, though.

The third time was in late summer time, after the discovery that I had been fooled a second time, this time by a lawyer. I called the psychiatric clinic and was advised to come right away to the hospital. I told the doctor there that I had been the victim of fraud another time. I was totally heart-broken, was crying almost hysterically. The doctor advised me to stay at the clinic for some days, and I agreed to that. I hadn't told my husband of this second fraud yet, I was terrified at the thought of telling him. I trembled when I remembered how angry and sad he had been the first time in March when it had become necessary to tell him the truth. We might have to split up definitely. When there is no trust between husband and wife, it is difficult to make the marriage work. A nurse called my husband and told him I had been taken care of at the hospital. He didn't ask anything, and I didn't tell him about the new fraud in my texted messages. I dared not. I felt so ashamed.

One day I had a talk with the doctor at the ward. He started our conversation saying "Now you have to accept that everything you have gone through these months is solely a matter of scam. There was never an officer in the U.S. army and there is no barrister now, there is just one or possibly two swindlers. They will go on asking for more and more money, as long as you meet their wishes." I didn't protest since I felt I had no strong arguments against this, there was no good reason to describe it as something else than swindle. "You should stay here over the weekend to calm down and stabilize your feelings", the doctor said. I stayed at the ward some days longer than the first two times I was treated for my crisis reaction. I was allowed to take walks in the area around the hospital, not to go downtown. I felt restless all the days I was staying there, brooding all the time on how to tell Sven this last horrible thing. On one of the next days I told him in a message, though. He answered he didn't know how to cope with this new mess.

SEARCHING FOR LEGAL HELP

I needed legal assistance from someone who could help me get useful information about the American officer, his lawyer and all the things that were of importance in this case. What institution in the U.S. is responsible for the national registration? Where could you get information about the residence of a certain citizen in the U.S.? At the end of March, I got in touch with a Swedish law firm on Internet. I explained my situation to them, and a lawyer promised she would try to help me. We talked on the phone about the problem with the American. She said it was common these days to use social media the way Anderson had. She didn't claim this had to be a case of fraud, but she said it most likely was. She said I had better ask for an American lawyer's assistance, since this man lived in the U.S. She contacted a lawyer's firm in Baltimore who promised to assist me in this matter. However, after a few weeks the American lawyer announced that she couldn't take on this assignment. She never gave a proper reason for her decision. It was another setback for me, and I spent hours on end to search for lawyers in Baltimore that could help me. Since I know that American lawyers charge a lot money for their work, I explained in my introductory letters that I could not pay for hourly worked time in advance, but I would compensate them with a large percentage of the repayment from the American, if this assignment would be carried out in a successful manner. I got no response from the lawyers I contacted. Other legal authorities that might have the mandate to maintain a client's interests towards an American citizen were also contacted, but I failed to get useful information anywhere.

Where should I make complaints about Anderson's fraud against me? From the correspondence at the beginning of our acquaintance I had learnt that he was employed by the DPKO, the Department of Peace-Keeping Operations, which allegedly was a department of the United Nations. Who is the head of the DPKO? I had asked the official at the Recess Department about this, but he never answered that question. He mentioned the government in the U.S. as accountable for their activity.

I found the website for DPKO, there was also a Police Unit in the organization, but there was no information about crimes of the kind I had been the victim of. I could find no relevant email addresses. I decided to write an ordinary letter to the head of the DPKO. The name of the highest official of DPKO was Jean-Pierre Lacroix. I spent some hours on writing a letter to Mr. Lacroix, presenting facts about the American officer who had swindled me of more than 100,000 euros. I asked Mr. Lacroix to respond to my letter.

I didn't get an answer this time, but when I a few months later wrote another letter to ask about the authenticity of some documents from U.S. Interpol, I received an e-letter from the Conduct and Discipline Unit, the Department of Field Service, United Nations. In this letter, they regretted very much that I had been targeted for fraud. I was also told that there was no one with the name Edward Anderson who worked for the DPKO in United Nations. Neither was there a Recess Department within the UN!

It was difficult for me to accept this information. I didn't trust them completely. I had received so many letters from the Recess Department who had introduced themselves as working as a Secret Service for DPKO. I concluded this meant that the official corporation, DPKO, had a certain department that was so secret, that they would not admit that it existed. I thought they did so in order to cover this part of the military activities. They should know something about their activity.

I was determined to do whatever I could, to make Edward Anderson pay for what he had done to me. At the same time, I struggled with emotions saying that he might be the one he said he was, that he really wanted to compensate me financially for all the expenses I had had for him. Maybe he had been overwhelmed by all the problems from the time he was imprisoned in London and detained there against his will. He might be just a very careless but honest man. He had no control of his economy, that was one thing for sure. But he must have been aware of the fact that he hadn't paid his taxes, when he contacted me on Facebook. He must have known that he had a muddled economy, when he asked for more and more loans from me. He might have thought I was cool enough to endure in this endless money mess.

I wondered whom or what institution I could turn to, to receive some information about Anderson. The authority accountable for national registration in Sweden is Skatteverket, a counterpart to the IRS in the U.S. All citizens of Sweden have a registration number, that is specific for him or her. I had earlier been in touch with the IRS about Mr. Anderson, but they would not answer my questions because I didn't know his Social Security Number. The Recess Department didn't want to give me any information about him either. When I asked them about Anderson, they referred to the Government.

I tried to accept the fact that I would never get back anything of all the money I had invested in the salvation of Anderson. It was extremely difficult! I thought I would have to divorce from my husband and start a new life in poverty. My situation was unbearable. No journeys abroad, no buffer for unforeseen expenses, nothing. It is the normal thing for most people in the world, but it isn't for me, living in a modern Western society. I'll not be able to keep the same level as my friends.

THE LAST MESSAGES
FROM EDWARD

A t the very last day of April, when we celebrated the advent of Spring by lighting big bonfires and "singing in spring", I got a puzzling message from Edward. I had wondered why he hadn't written any messages to me the last weeks. Maybe he had accepted the fact that I couldn't help him more financially? I didn't miss the messages, but I was somehow curious about his life. Had he been informed of my letter to the Head of the Department for Peace-Keeping Operations?

Every town and village have their own celebrations around the bonfire on April 30, no matter if there is snow and it's cold, which often is the case, at least in large parts of Sweden. One thing for sure is that days have become much longer at this time of the year, and some spring flowers have arrived. We went to a place close to a beautiful lake where there was an open celebration of Last April Day.

The second last message he sent on April 30 had this content: "I just need a little help. That is all I desire. You have hurt me deeply." The next day, May 1, his message was: "Please, talk to me please". I never did. What should I have said? I could have told him how depressed he had made me, how seriously he had damaged my economy and my social life. I could have said that he had ruined my life. I am usually honest, but sometimes honesty is not the best policy. I had the feeling he was very depressed and lonely, and I was not able to cheer him up. He had never shown that he really cared for me. He ignored my pleas for some help from him. When my husband had been informed about the loans to him, and when I realized how much I was encumbered in debts, I asked him to send some money back to me, because my situation was unbearable. He never answered! Only once at the end of our acquaintance he said he would try to send me money at the end of the week, if his friend kept his promise to him. He had gone "wide and far" to find the money. I take it his friend didn't keep his promise, because I never received money from him.

It was a wonderful weather this day. The sky was clear, the water in the lake was gleaming, it was warm enough to be outdoors without being cold. There was a chorus singing songs about spring, and a speech to spring was held. But all the time I was thinking of Edward and the message he had sent. I wondered why he had been hurt. Had he got a telling-off from someone at the top of his organization? Was he hurt because I hadn't conceded to his wishes about more money?

At the middle of May, I found his messages to me on Facebook had been taken away. I then deleted him from my list of friends on the Facebook account, but I couldn't delete him from my mind. I constantly asked myself questions about what had happened to him. Had he been forced by the police or a superior of the military organization to stop using Facebook? Or had he himself come to the conclusion that he had no use for me anymore?

CONTACTING THE
SWEDISH POLICE

The first advice you probably would give anyone who has been victimized like me, would be to call the police. The police, if any authority, are those that investigate crimes that people are exposed to. While being thrilled by criminal stories in reality and in fiction, I realize that policemen very rarely live up to the capacity to solve crimes committed, as they do in those documentary programs about crimes, or in fictional detective novels. In real life, you seldom come across that very skilled, committed police detective who confronts the perpetrator and makes him (mostly men) give himself away. That brilliant detective or attorney who spares no pains to uncover complicated crimes is rare.

The Swedish police has undergone a major reorganization in recent years, which in practice has involved a centralization of the resources. The reform has been severely criticized by both the staff themselves and by the public. While it is difficult to measure police efficacy, it is an undeniable fact that they don't cope to solve many crimes of this kind within a reasonable time.

I was very reluctant to turn to the local police even though I had been advised to do so by the American Embassy in Stockholm, the police in Baltimore and by a friend whom I had entrusted my situation to. I feared they would not pay much attention to my "story".

My fears turned out to be well motivated, when I visited the police station next to my home one day in May. The police officer I had the opportunity to talk to for about ten minutes, told me right away that the man I believed I had been in touch with as a Facebook friend, was a fraudster, possibly living in the same town that was next to my home. I suppose his gut feeling was enough for him to dismiss me as one of the many people who are fooled by fraudsters who promise big revenues. He compared me to someone giving a loan of 100 crowns to a friend, and then wants this money back. "You cannot go to the police to get your money back!" In his opinion I most likely was a naïve person to believe that this story ever could be settled and that the perpetrator would be arrested and sentenced. He didn't take the trouble of getting through my material that I had collected to give all the information available. He was going to finish his work that day and had only a few minutes to spare for me. Although I had little hopes that the police would help me, I was very disappointed when I heard him talking.

My police report had been registered, but a short time later I received a letter from the Police saying that there would be no investigation of the crime, since the criminal act had not been committed in Sweden. There was information in the letter as to how this decision could be appealed against to the police authority above the local police. My husband read the letter and said the case had not been handled properly. But to appeal to the police authority in Jönköping would probably not be of any use, he said.

Though I felt somehow forlorn, I some days later wrote a letter to the Police authority in Jönköping formulating the reasons why this case should be investigated into. I pointed out that this cyber fraud was not committed in one specific country, Facebook exists in all the world, and the activity of fraud was carried out in several countries. The individuals that took part in this case were both in Sweden and in Syria, Great Britain and the U.S. The victim is a Swedish citizen, which is of vital importance. The size of the amount stolen was so high that it could not be deemed irrelevant as a police matter.

While staying in a ward of the psychiatric clinic, I was called by a policeman from the local office some weeks later. The policeman informed me that my appeal had been accepted and a certain police detective would deal with this case. It was good news for me in this desperate situation, but I didn't get overjoyed, because I felt that this was still a very small step in the right direction. The police are overloaded with reports of crimes they will never be able to deal with. I just hoped for a telephone call or email from the police detective that would give me some information about Anderson. I wanted to know if he was serving a prison term or not, if he was known by the police before for other crimes, or what else there was known about him.

I wanted to receive some concrete and true information about Edward Anderson. To this end I contacted the Police in Baltimore and reported the fraud on an Internet form. I asked if they could confirm that Edward was a citizen of Baltimore. I enclosed the picture from the passport photo that Edward had sent to me. I immediately received an answer from a police official saying "no" but no more. I asked if this answer meant that the person wasn't a citizen of Baltimore. He answered "No, it means I am not able to confirm this." He advised me to report to the next local police. I did so, though I had low expectations that they would do anything to help me.

As a consequence of the centralization of the police, telephone calls from the public are managed by a central telephone exchange for all police offices in Sweden. It is next to impossible to get in touch directly with the officer you want to talk to. I chose to write email to the police detective in charge of my police report. I asked him politely to request some information from the police in Baltimore about the man called Edward Anderson, since the local police there had refused to give any information about him to me.

The policeman in charge of my case answered however that he had no plans to get in touch with the Baltimore police. He was quite sure that there was a mastermind in this business whom I didn't know the name of. When I later contacted him about the lawyer in London who offered his services, he gave me the same answer: I was fooled by scammers, and that was the whole thing. The district attorney would later decide if it was worthwhile to investigate this fraud further.

THE BARRISTER GEOFFREY NELSON CONTACTS ME

I was almost constantly thinking of Anderson and wondered what had happened to him. Was everything he had told me lies? What was his real name? I regretted very much I had not backed out of this business when Edward had arrived in London and was sent to prison. That was the first time I had a strong reason to be suspicious of him. My thoughts about him were sometimes optimistic, when I managed to convince myself that he some day in the future would pay back what he owed me. I couldn't stop hoping for him to do the right thing and pay back.

In May, I received mail from Geoffrey Nelson, the lawyer who had represented Anderson in the London Court, and reportedly had done so well that Anderson was released from custody. He asked me if I wanted to have some new information about Anderson. I said of course yes, and he told me that Edward had been arrested and was now serving his time in prison, because he had refused to pay taxes for several years. Nelson said it was possible for me to get back the money I had lent to Anderson, if I sent all the receipts of my bank transactions and a copy of the passport photo that Anderson had sent to me. Nelson himself had given him a loan, and would now send in a document concerning his loan. Would I like to have his assistance in this errand? Sure, I did! There was however a snag in it – I had to pay upfront 14,000 euros. What in detail the money was intended for he didn't say, but the U.S. Army had reportedly consented to pay back what Anderson had borrowed from me. He assured me it would be easy for him to handle the request for compensation, and within a week or two the money would be there for me. It was 100% certain!

I had to resign, because I had no money left for anything more, but I suggested he would get this amount of money *after* he had successfully done this job and I had the money on my bank account. He answered he would gladly have lent me this money, but he was himself out of cash, and had to pay for his own request. He couldn't help me this way. I dropped this opportunity to get back what I had lost in the project "save Anderson". I reminded him to send the document concerning Anderson's judgement from the money laundering process in London. He dismissed my plea sounding very irritated. I should think of other more relevant things, and accept his offer to handle my loans to Anderson!

I didn't trust Mr. Nelson. He claimed to be a barrister, but when I asked the Bar Council in London they told me his name was not included in their registry for barristers in England and Wales. *Barrister* is a title that is protected by Law against abuse of it. He seemed to be a lawyer of a more doubtful character. But he might also be a common lawyer, who only helps his clients to get the lowest possible penalty or to be acquitted. I was painfully uncertain if he was honest enough to help me in this situation.

There was a mention of *auction* in Nelson's letter. The information he gave was always vague and scanty. Maybe the legal authorities in Baltimore would sell Anderson's property on an auction to collect the balance from the tax debts? Nelson was anything but clear in his short messages to me. But the sheer possibility that he really was able to help me get back money made me puzzled, even though I didn't agree to pay this money. I didn't have the means to do so, and my husband would of course refuse to lend money for this purpose. He got very angry when I told him about the lawyer's offer to help me.

When I heard from the "kind" lawyer in August again, I was more responsive to his suggestions. He said that he was a custodian of Law, and he wanted me to apply for money from the army. He would help me. This time he spelt his name consistently with one *f.* He asked me if I had got back the money I had lent to Anderson, because he himself had received the money Anderson had borrowed from him. I asked if it was the Defense Department or DPKO that had paid back. The latter he answered very shortly. It was a pity that I hadn't received my money, he wrote. He wanted me to smile again. This phrase reminded me of Edward, who also had wanted to put a smile on my face again. He had failed miserably to do so. Nelson's words were beautiful music to my ears. The hope to regain my economic safety was awakened. I was light of heart again for some days.

Nelson contacted me on the telephone on some occasions. Once he called me while staying in Turkey waiting to collect the money that I would transfer to a Turkish bank account. My cell phone was then lying close to where my husband was sitting. He took the cellphone, noticing that the phone call was from Turkey. He became very suspicious and asked me what kind of acquaintances I had in Turkey. I pretended I didn't know who was calling from Turkey. I couldn't take the phone calls on such occasions. I learned to put the cell phone on the soundless position when my husband was in the house. I couldn't tell him about my contacts with Nelson.

When I talked with Nelson on the phone he was soft and compassionate, but I didn't catch every word he said, because I was extremely nervous and he spoke in a low voice. He showed great empathy with me. He would give me a surprise, he said. "A good surprise?" I asked. He said it would be a very nice surprise. He told me that Anderson was "nowhere to be found", since he had been bailed out by an aunt. He had been released, but had not returned to the prison. The Intelligence was searching him now.

This time he wanted 3,730 euros upfront to start the process. This was really not so much, considering what I had been made to lend to Anderson before. But it was a problem for me, since I had no reserve to take money from. I tried to scrape together all I had left from my salary account. There were some 18,000 crowns (10 crowns ≈ 1 euro). I suggested to Nelson that I pay half the sum he wanted – 1,865 euros – and pay back the rest *after* the money from the U.S. Army had been paid back to me, i.e. when I could see the money on my bank account. In addition, he would then get 10% of the whole sum Anderson had borrowed from me. I hoped this would motivate Nelson to do his best for me. Ten percent meant a nice little sum of about 10,800 euros for him. He agreed after what seemed to be some hesitation, and sent an agreement form where the terms for his assistance were written down and signed by him. I printed the agreement form and signed it, scanned it and sent back by email to the lawyer. I transferred the fee of 1,865 euros to a Turkish account.

A few hours later, Nelson announced that Interpol demanded I pay upfront 15% taxes of the total amount reserved for me. They needed to receive this sum before they transferred the money that was reserved for me. Nelson assured me that he had tried to persuade the U.S. Interpol into making an exception for me, but they had refused.

15 percent was in this case equal to about 15,000 euros, which I didn't possess. Nelson said it was urgent to raise this money as soon as possible.

I had tantalizing pangs when I considered the fact that "only" 15,000 was needed to attain my goal, and to restore my economy and peace of mind. Tantalus was a Greek mythological figure, most famous for his eternal punishment never to reach what he wanted so very much: He was made to stand in a pool of water beneath a fruit tree with low branches. Every time he tried to grasp a fruit, the fruit eluded his hand, and likewise the water always receded when he tried to take a drink. Every time I thought I was close to a "happy end", there was a new hindrance, the demand for a large sum, that stopped me from reaching this goal. In this way, I had tried to put an end to Edward's endless financial problems time after time. I just had to find this money from somewhere! I was very excited when I thought I would get back what I had lost. I made a new search for loans on Internet, and I was after some days offered a loan on a new bank. A few days later this money arrived with my bank account. I started to write a wish list of all the things I really needed and would soon be able to buy. 15,000 euros is on the whole a small amount, isn't it? I was so very happy when I thought everything would be fine again.

After a couple of days, however, I was struck by a terrible setback, when Nelson sent a long email with attached copies of U.S. Interpol's notification letter to him. The notification letter stated that the 15% tax was a typographical mistake. The correct percentage was 50% of the total sum they were to transfer to his client. This meant I would have to add another 37,000 euros before I could receive my money! Nelson deeply regretted this mistake, pointing out that he had tried to persuade the official on Interpol to make an exception for me, since I had suffered so long a time for this American citizen. But they insisted on their conditions. My mood sank low again when I learnt this. I read the attached letters from Interpol and Nelson; in one letter, he blamed them for being incompetent. It all seemed very trustworthy. The official who wrote the letter from U.S. Interpol used the address *usa.com* as domain. The language showed many clumsy wordings, it was the same style that was characteristic of Nelson's messages.

They tried to soften the message by saying that 85% of the taxes could be refunded from the IRS, if the lawyer made a formal appeal. Fine, but why this vicious circle of money? Why couldn't they instead make a deduction from the amount of money before they paid back the money to me? Nelson explained that this system had worked well for many years in the United States, I just had to accept the rules.

The big problem was again: How would I be able to raise the money, now this huge amount of 37,810 euros – a fortune I never have been close to having saved on a bank account. Would there be a bank that granted me such a high sum of money, encumbered with debts that I already was? I was terrified at the thought that I would burden my economy with yet another loan. I made a new search on Internet for a loan of 370,000 crowns. I got only one hit this time, the same bank that had given me a big loan earlier. This loan had been redeemed by my husband after he had heard about the bank loans for Anderson. I told myself it would just be for a very short time I had this loan. It would be a true pleasure to pay back all the loans! It would be marvelous to pay back to my husband what he had sacrificed for me. The sooner I could gather the money and pay the taxes for Interpol, the sooner all the bank loans would be redeemed. After some days, the new money arrived with my bank account.

I was extremely nervous about this last transaction. What would happen if Nelson after all was a fraudster? I dared not think of the consequences. I asked Nelson to give me some proof that he really was a trustworthy barrister. A diploma of his examination, a passport or some certificate that showed me he was the one he claimed to be. He seemed a bit annoyed at this request, but he sent a copy of his passport. The photo of him in this passport was a spitting image of an actor who has played the role of James Bond. There were some details in this passport that weren't consistent with the information he had given about himself before, but I was too stressful to confront him with this inconsistency at this moment.

The bank had reacted to my former money transaction to a Turkish bank account, and asked me if I knew the account holder. I told Nelson about this and he gave me another bank account to transfer the money into. This time it was the same bank that I used myself for all everyday transactions. Only a first name was given, Annette, no surname for the account holder. I suppose this was a way to protect the privacy of the agent who was entrusted the task to transfer money. Nelson wouldn't risk that I recognized the account holder personally. It made the transfer much easier for me too, but it was such a high amount, that I had to call the bank official to accomplish the transfer. The official asked me again if I knew the receiver, and this time I lied and said Yes.

The following weekend we had guests in our house, and my sister visited us right after our friends had left. It was a terrible strain to my nerves to socialize with our friends and my sister while waiting for the money to arrive on a bank account and move on in this business. My sister knew that something was wrong with me. I had made her understand that I had troubles, but I hadn't told her about the nature of my problems. She knew that something bad had happened in my life that had made me depressed. I had not been able to talk with her on the phone for months. The same day she arrived I made the final money transaction to "Annettes" bank account. While I tried my best to be a good hostess, I trembled with anguish, I sweated profusely and I felt very tense all the time.

When my sister had arrived with us, I had to do some shopping in the town next to our property. Throughout the time I was shopping, I thought about the large money transfer I had made. I was unable to focus on anything else. I made some mistakes due to my absentmindedness. I was in a grocery store and bought a lot of food, but left the food articles behind, that I had paid for at the counter. It took some hours before I even noticed that I had left the food behind in the shop. But when I eventually was planning the next day's dinner, I got aware of my mistake. I told my sister and husband about the mistake, and jumped into my car to go back to the shop where I bought the provisions. My body was wet with sweat, my heart felt heavy. A shop assistant had gathered my food stuff into a bag in the shop. When at home, I heard from my husband that my sister had tried to make him tell her what had happened to me. He didn't though. He is a man of his word.

I don't know how I coped with my anxiety those days, but I had some sedative medicine that helped me to keep up appearances. I was like a zombie, didn't really hear what my guests said. I felt so sad, downhearted as if I knew that the total disaster was to happen. I never trusted Nelson completely, but still I felt I had to set my last hopes to him. There was no other option for me.

Nelson sent messages to me about his plans to go to Interpol in the U.S. and finish the business for me. He would keep me posted over the whole process.

He soon reported some difficulties to make withdrawals from the bank account in Turkey. It was such a high amount of money the bank officials had said. They could not deliver all the money at one time. But there was no need to worry, he assured me, he knew how to handle this business! It would only take some days more to get hold of all the money.

The same day as Nelson had arrived in the United States and was to settle the business with Interpol, he sent a message about a credit card that didn't work for him, he was so "disappointed". He had used the money I had transferred for the taxes. Could I send him the balance of 8,000 euros?

This was like a hard slap in my face! I was fortunately enough alone, when I got the message. I felt right away this message was the conclusive proof that he was a fraudster, not a savior, as I had hoped. He knew that my economy was severely strained by these last transactions that he and the U.S. Interpol had made me pay. He knew I was in a very difficult situation. He was no better than Anderson had been. I took a long walk into the forest, I sat down in the grass and on stubbles crying. I had an intense feeling of disaster. I had been swindled a second time! I was in a desperate situation again. I wished I was able to commit suicide. I went home and made lunch as usual, after the lunch I told my husband that there was something I had to do in town. I called the psychiatric clinic I had been a patient to before, and was given an appointment to a doctor right away. I was in hospital for the next five days. I was terribly afraid to tell my husband about this second fraud.

It had thus turned out that Nelson had no noble motivations to help at all, he just wanted to siphon off as much money as possible from me. He would never see to it that my money was paid back to me. His kindness had been false.

I told Nelson that I had no money left to send to him, and he, if anyone, should know that well! I told him he had used dirty confidence tricks with me. He had contacted me at a very sensitive point when I was vulnerable and needed comfort from somebody. I had been an easy target for this kind of foul play. Nelson answered that I insulted him. What offense had he done to me to deserve these insults? He emphasized what an awful lot of work he had done to help me, and that I hadn't paid him a cent for this. My last words to him in this exchange of reproaches were "You will be punished one day". These words were sent to him while I was taken care of at the emergency ward at the hospital. He protested, "For what? What is your problem madam?" He regretted ever having offered me help.

When I asked Nelson to send back the 56,000 euros for the taxes I had transferred to him, he was very reluctant, suggesting he give the money to someone I knew in the U.S. He said he might stay in the U.S. for a month or more to deal with a new case. It would take a long time before he could transfer the money, i.e. the rest of money after his expenses had been paid. Why transferring money from the U.S. to me would be so difficult for him, he didn't say. He never gave a statement of his accounts to me. I just had to accept that the money had dwindled into 40,000 euros. He had somehow used 16,000 euros for himself. That was certainly not in accordance with the deal we had made!

Why did a man like him –who pretends to be a well-educated man– steal money from his own client? I had taken the risk to use him as my legal representative, even though I had some reason to distrust him. How did he get this arrogant, disrespectful attitude to people who entrusted him with important tasks? How could a lawyer enjoy life without being honest to his clients? The simple answer is of course that money makes life enjoyable enough to ignore the remorse it might cause. Money stands for safety, power, liberty, a chance to enjoy a good living standard. Some people earn their living by stealing from other people, even if they don't admit they do.

Was Geoffrey Nelson a child from a struggling family; had he been envious of other young buddies from better living conditions? Did he revenge himself on me? Maybe he thought that I could easily regain balance in my finances. He was kind to me before I made the money transactions for the Interpol taxes. He had now siphoned off all the money I could gather, and made me even more encumbered with debts than before. I realized that I had wasted my last hopes on a man without a conscience. Probably he thought that it served me right to be destitute of money. I had to take the consequences of my stupidity.

FRANTIC EFFORTS TO
REGAIN MONEY

I asked myself if there was anything I could do to regain the money I had lost, since Nelson had failed to do his duty. I turned to the Recess Department and asked them if they could recommend a good lawyer whom I could turn to with my case. They answered by giving three names of lawyers who had been successful. One of them was Cindy Flynn, who allegedly also was a professor of Law. I mailed to her and presented my case for her.

She answered very soon, saying she had contacted the Army about this matter, and an official there had told her that they had closed the file and deposited the money intended for me with Interpol. They should forward the money to me. One of her best friends was the head of Interpol and he had confirmed that this money was kept by them. She also confirmed that I would have to pay 50% taxes of the total amount upfront. A large part, 80-85% of the taxes, would later be refunded if I submitted a formal application, made by a legal representative. I had seen that document about taxes that Nelson had attached in his message, but there was no mention of my name in this document. I could not decide if it was authentic or not. And I wasn't sure if this rule really applied to my case. Cindy Flynn assured me the document was authentic, but my husband was convinced it was a fake document, and told me this was not the usual way a corporation like Interpol would act. The correct way is to inform the person who is the receiver of a certain economic compensation in the first place. To demand that the receiver should pay half the amount in taxes before the compensation was paid back was very strange. The whole process was absurd, he said and I agreed. At this time, I was so full of distrust and suspicion against almost everyone I was in touch with. I did not even trust my own judgement anymore.

I had some difficult time when I didn't know whom I should trust more: my husband or the barrister Cindy and the Recess Department. I wasn't sure if Sven had told me the whole truth about Interpol. At one moment, I felt my husband just screwed it up by his doubts concerning the authenticity of the documents. Some moments later I felt he was right. I had never heard of a legal process like this before.

Barrister Cindy said she would charge me 6,000 euros to represent me at Interpol, and I would of course have to add to the amount she had in charge to make it 52,000 euros in all. I found the barrister's fee quite affordable, but I told her that my husband, who actually is a lawyer, didn't support me in paying these taxes. Sixteen thousand euros of the original 56,000 euros were missing, since Nelson had used this money for other purposes and left me in the lurch. He had not acted in accordance with the deal we both had agreed to. I was at a loss what to do. Whom could I really trust?

When I talked with Sven, my husband, about the terms that were set up for me, he was sure that they were all scamming me. This second barrister was, according to him, most likely a fraudster too. The Recess Department was also part of this scamming net. I should not answer to their messages at all! I should be quiet and passive, he said. He advised me to use a very harsh language to them in a last message. But I wasn't able to do so, I wouldn't burn all my bridges. I was still hoping for a solution in one way or another.

His standpoint filled me with anguish, since I believed or hoped that Cindy Flynn was an honest, professional person. She had pointed out to me that her friend was the head of Interpol, which would be helpful for me. But I could not afford a third fraud, and I could not take a new loan. I would not be granted another loan.

Cindy Flynn got angry with me, when I told her that I would probably not be able to pay the money needed for this process. I asked her to transfer the 40,000 euros that Nelson had handed over to her, to my bank account and make a deduction of 500 euros for the transmission cost. I gave her the necessary information about my bank account. I needed the money badly, I told her. "Do you think I am a servant for you?" she responded. She called my behavior childish, and said she would report me to the Police and to the Recess Department. She suspected some sort of conspiracy against her, that I was in cahoots with Nelson to ruin her "carrier" (*career*)!

Was it all just foul play against me? Did Cindy Flynn and Geofrey Nelson belong to a network of fraudsters or unscrupulous lawyers? I believe they did. They probably passed on their victims to each other when something got wrong.

Before I told Cindy that I had to drop the case, she tried her best to encourage my efforts to gather as much money as was needed for Interpol to pay back the 104,000 euros. She asked a provocative question, "Why don't you want to receive the money that is ready for you. It is 100% certain!" Nelson had expressed himself in the same way, but in his action, he had shown this was far from certain. They both seemed to believe that anybody could get any amount of money they wanted.

I tried to find some logic in this lengthy procedure, but I failed. I know through my husband, who earlier was a tax lawyer, that the tax office has a difficult task collecting taxes from individuals and companies. But why couldn't they just make a deduction for the taxes from the total amount they would send to me? It didn't make sense that I, the victimized person, had to pay taxes before I received the money that I had been deprived of by dishonest people. I was too poor to get compensation for the money that had been taken from me! I had been suspicious about this process throughout the time Nelson was engaged as my lawyer. Finally, I had more or less resigned and paid the money that was required. There are many strange rules you don't understand, I thought.

Sven advised me to ask the Interpol office in Stockholm if there really was some money reserved for me. I doubted they would be forthcoming to me. They would hardly bother to answer my question. But at that moment I didn't have the strength and courage to oppose his views. We wrote a short letter to the Interpol section in Stockholm asking them to confirm if there really was money reserved for me. We asked if the notification letter was genuine.

Sven got a phone call from the Police in Stockholm who cooperates with Interpol, that had told him that the notification letter was not from the real Interpol. It was a fake, and the policeman had told him that there had been other people who had been fooled this way. The barrister Cindy must have lied to me when she had confirmed the authenticity of the document. It took some time before I realized that. It was extremely painful to accept this. I completely broke down.

U.S. INTERPOL AND THE RECESS DEPARTMENT

To assure myself about the authenticity of the notification letter that I had received from U.S. Interpol, I had written an ordinary letter to Interpol in Washington, attaching copies of the notification letter and of Nelson's passport. I asked them if these documents were authentic and trustworthy.

I was obviously in touch with two different branches of Interpol, if not with one authentic and one false. The first Interpol sent notification letters to my lawyers Nelson and Flynn. They had also sent me an e-letter, informing me that if I didn't pay the taxes before October 5, the money would go back to the Army. I answered I had already paid the taxes through Nelson, and implied they probably knew that the "barrister" Nelson was a fraudster. They didn't return to me anymore.

The other Interpol that is part of the Justice Department in Washington sent me an e-letter telling me that the notification letter to barrister Cindy and me was an illegitimate document. They also confirmed that Nelson's passport was false. The name in the signature had been clarified. The letter was signed by the General Counsel Kevin R. Spacey. The language used in the letter was, unlike the language in the notification letters, correct and clear.

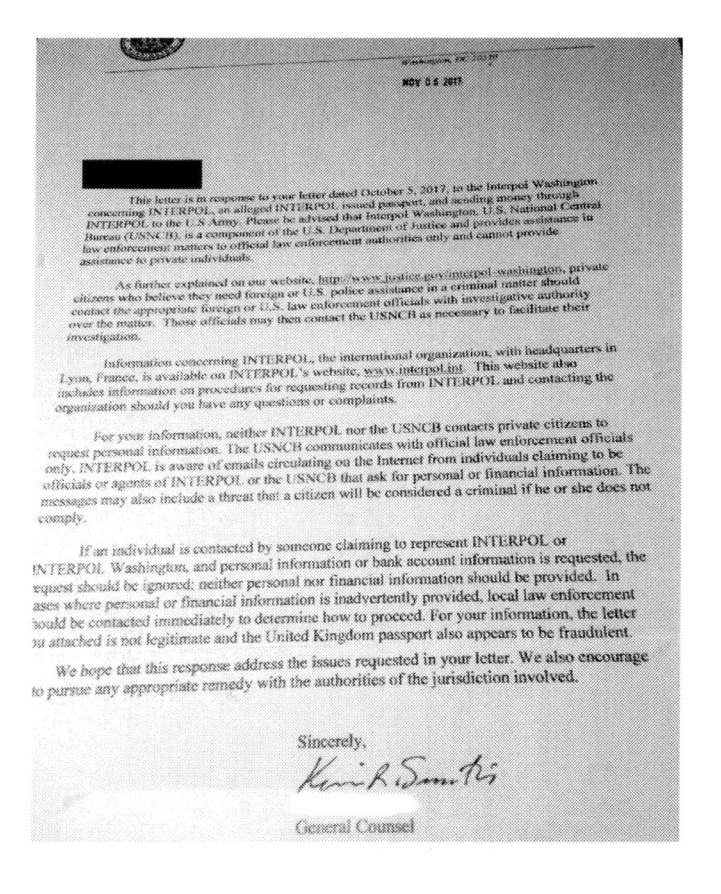

They explained in the letter that Interpol never contacts private individuals. However, they did not say, in plain text, that the documents I had received came from a false authority. They said the documents were not "legitimate", i.e. conforming to the law or to rules. It might mean that the officials who wrote the documents were not authorized to send such documents. They also confirmed my suspicion that Nelson's passport was a fake.

Some days later I got mail from The Recess Department where they regretted that I had insulted both the U.S. Interpol and barrister Cindy by talking about fraud in my messages to them. I should control my anger, they said. I now had to hire a new lawyer to represent me vis-à-vis Interpol in order to receive the money. The last day to request it was October 5. So, I had to give up my hopes of getting back money! I had no means whatsoever to meet these requirements.

Some week later an official at The Recess Department told me that Anderson had been arrested again and taken to court, where he had admitted to having collected money from me. The judge of the court wanted this case to be finished off. They reminded me that I should hire a lawyer who made a formal request to the U.S. Interpol. What should I do? I wasn't able to hire another American lawyer. I came to the conclusion I had to give a strong statement to the Recess Department myself. I knew that my husband, the lawyer, would not do this, he wouldn't even respond to this message.

I wrote a long letter where I emphasized that I had been put in an absurd situation by their demands to pay taxes. At the end, I referred to the Independence Declaration saying that we "are endowed by [our] Creator with certain unalienable Rights, that among these are Life, Liberty and the pursuit of Happiness." I wrote that I would go on fighting for my right to enjoy a pleasant life with the savings from my professional life. I would fight to the last drop of blood. It might sound pathetic, but it was my true intention.

The official at the Recess Department answered they wanted me to calm down. They would investigate this matter but they needed 40 working days to do so. After this period, they would transfer both the 104,000 euros for Anderson and the 40,000 euros that Nelson had given to Cindy Flynn. "That sounds good", I answered. But I feared it was too good to be true.

When eight weeks had passed, I sent a new letter to the Recess Department, reminding them they had promised to pay back what I had lost in this case. They answered that I had to pay taxes before they could transfer the money, the same amount of money that the U.S. Interpol had asked for –52,000 euros! The money that I after great efforts managed to collect, and which Nelson and Flynn had embezzled!

This answer made me very upset, since I had told them about my difficult financial situation. They knew how much I had paid to Anderson and Nelson, and still they wanted me to apply for another bank loan! It was of course impossible for me. I pointed out to them how strange it was that I had to raise money for something they were accountable for. They had been couriers to Anderson eleven times, bringing him the money I transferred for different purposes. They never protested to those many transactions of money to him. When I later asked if they could tip me about a good lawyer they had given me Nelson's name the first time, and Flynn's the second time I was troubled. Both lawyers had refused to pay back anything. I insisted on their sending me the money, at least the amount of 40,000 euros that Cindy Flynn had been in charge of.

I was now told that Nelson had been arrested and sentenced to 15 years in jail because of his dishonesty. The Recess Department had also received reports from other persons about Nelson's dishonesty. This was confusing for me. It didn't sound credible to me that Nelson was in jail. It usually takes much longer than two months to have a man arrested and sentenced for fraud. Both Anderson and Nelson had been sent to jail, when they stopped communicating with me.

The official at The Recess Department sent me a message saying that I must understand that they were not "in the possession of 40,000 euros". He maybe said too much this time. "How would you then be able to pay the 140,000 euros to me, if you can't transfer 40,000 euros", I answered. He didn't answer.

Cindy was innocent, he said, but she had left the 40,000 euros that Nelson handed over to her, at "the station" saying that they should give it to Nelson, and he had retrieved the money later. This didn't add up to me at all. I had told Cindy about Nelson's dishonest character; I had told her that he had stolen 16,000 euros from me. That was why I had turned to her and asked her to help me. What barrister would hand over money to a thief like that?

There was much to suggest that the Recess Department was the mastermind behind all these fraudulent actions against me. When Nelson had done his part to drain me of my money, they directed me to another "barrister" to go on pressing me for money.

THE TRUTHS ABOUT
ANDERSON AND THE REST

There are two theories about this fraud. The theory that my husband and the Swedish police find most trustworthy is that the American officer was no officer in reality, but a simple cheater who contacted me, and he was part of a scamming net. The perpetrators have tried to catch some kind person to siphon off his or her money. Kind people who want to help are the most profitable people, if it concerns a matter of charity. They can make sacrifices to help, and, if necessary, the scammer can make them believe they will finally get back the money they have transferred to them. Anderson, Nelson, MacMillan, Flynn, the people behind Recess Department and one of the branches of the U.S. Interpol seemed to be parts of a scamming activity. They seemed to cooperate to make the victims believe they are trustworthy persons and corporations. This type of fraud is particularly common in the case of major accidents that affect the population in a place or country, such as the earthquake in Haiti in 2010 or the tsunami in Thailand in 2004.

What supports this theory are the many common features in their way of communicating with me. They all use the same kind of colloquial language in their messages. Some phrases are recurring in their language: "I want to put a smile in your face", "It is 100% certain", "Respond urgently" and the like. All of them appear to be weak writers. They may use special words to economy or legal activity, but they fail to use a correct sentence structure. Some formal words and phrases are used, but the overall level of language is casual. They don't capitalize the first letter of names, they generally don't use punctuation marks, and they sometimes omit words that would make the sentences complete (and understandable). Many words are wrongly spelt. These mistakes in their language could be explained as typical of the sloppy language that most people use when they are in a hurry while writing. But it is not common, according to my knowledge and experience, for highly educated persons to make so frequent basic language errors.

Anderson's written English was far from correct. Some of his mistakes are typically made by a person who is very upset or in a great hurry. He often wrote long messages in a fit of anger or despair. Writing was not part of his profession. The sloppy English used by the "barristers" made me however suspicious. A barrister is a well-educated person, usually capable of expressing himself/herself well, both in speech and in writing. In some of the mail from Nelson, he used the language a person with English as a second language uses. For example, "don't worry your self" indicates he has not the genuine feeling for the English language. In his mother tongue the corresponding verb of *worry* is probably reflexive ('worry oneself') as it is in Swedish. It is a proof of imperfect command of English.

Their written language shows a type of language mistakes that indicate dyslexia. Edward's texts are by far the most numerous and seem to be genuine chat talk. Maria MacMillan wrote three e-letters, similar in style to heart-to-heart talk. Geoffrey Nelson's texts were more enigmatic, he omitted many words that would make his text coherent. I had to guess quite often what he really meant, I had to fill out with words that he probably meant to be there. In some cases, I did not understand what he really meant. I have no problems with the words connected to his profession. But the way he used the words was far from clear.

Being a university teacher of linguistics, I have met students from different walks of life. The language proficiency varies a lot even among people who work as teachers or have other jobs where they are expected to express themselves in a clear and correct way. Maria MacMillan was reportedly Anderson's son's teacher. She might be a teacher of Arithmetic, History, Home economics or any other subject. She is probably not a teacher of English. There are however only three letters from her to base my opinion on about her.

They used confidence tricks to make me feel relatively safe. I can discern different steps in their strategy. First, they choose suitable victims. Anderson probably searched on social media before he made his friend request to me. On Facebook, he could see what kind of interests I had. He once said he loved my profile picture, a picture where I'm holding a kitten in my hands. It was a very gentle picture of me. A woman who cares for animals may also be thoughtful of humans. He might have made friendly requests to other women as well, to see who would accept him as a friend. And I swallowed the bait.

Anderson's real name is probably not the one that is indicated in the passport copy he sent to me. The response from the American Embassy about an alteration in the passport implies there was something wrong about it. Moreover, he should have another surname if his father's name was the German name on the bank account. The Defense Department purports it was a case of impersonation of a man who served the U.S. Army. Anderson said at the very start of our friendship that he was an officer "under cover" in Syria. I guess that implies they use aliases instead of their real names.

The other persons in this plot could just hang on where Anderson had let me go. The lawyer and the teacher supported Anderson's demands by referring to his predicament. When I allowed them to get closer to me, they gained my confidence by their friendly "talk". Anderson asked me about my life, wanted me to send pictures of myself and the young people I met daily. He said comforting words when I had mentioned some problems I had in my job. The lawyer Nelson called me on the phone and was extremely soft-spoken when I was sad.

There were some critical moments in our communication, when they had to prove they were serious. When I hesitated to help him, Anderson gave me access to his personal bank account and his password, but I never managed to make withdrawals from this account. Nelson forwarded notification letters from Interpol with a special logo on top of the letters, to convince me that he didn't lie about the taxes I had to pay. There were critical points when I considered to drop the case, but Nelson first used hard words to make me move on in this process ("You must sign a document where you state that you will not claim any money. I have done my bit. You owe me the rest."), and later, when I bowed to his demands, he used soft words ("I really understand you. I want you to smile again"), but at the end, when I wasn't able to pay more, he was very rude with me ("You are a very big joker. I regret I offered you help."). Anderson likewise used both hard and soft words to me. When he had been harsh to me, he later asked my forgiveness. It all sounded so genuine. I let myself be lulled into feelings of security.

Nelson stands out as a very shady figure, not as the respectable barrister he stated he was. He never sent a copy of the judgement concerning Anderson, which also raises doubts about his authority. I asked him twice to send it. I have not been able to retrieve this document from the Court of London.

Yet another suspicious detail was the fact that the Bar of Council did not have Geoffrey Nelson in their registers of barristers in England and Wales. He might be a lawyer, but he was called 'barrister' in the letters from U.S. Interpol, and he called himself so. It goes against rules to use this title without authority.

Nelson made one mistake: his first and second names were indicated in the wrong boxes in his passport, if Nelson really was his surname, not the given name. His name according to the passport was Nelson Geofrey.

He wasn't truthful in any way. He would not have used the language he did to me, if he had been a well-educated gentleman. I was called "a big joker" when I asked him to transfer to me the money I had scraped together for the taxes. He gave no account of his spending almost 16,000 euros out of the 56,000 euros I transferred to him (via agents' bank accounts). He just used the money for private purposes, i.e. stole it from me. He showed no compassion with me this time.

What tells against this theory is my "gut feeling" that Anderson was an ordinary but very careless man. He said a lot of things that sounded trustworthy to me. His way of talking about himself sounded very genuine, and so did his fear to be arrested by the police. "They can track me down easily. I am scared to death they will take me", he said. He knew that he had done something wrong that he could be held responsible for. If this was the fraud against me, or a violation of military discipline, I don't know. I am well aware of the fact that this gut feeling I have concerning Anderson may be false. All successful cheaters make a serious impression. They know how to dupe people.

Why would he (and his companions) use this complicated way of cheating me? He *was* staying in London at a hotel, I know that for sure. I called the hotel staff using a phone number indicative of London, Great Britain. It beats me why he would use this way to ask for more and more money. It seems to be a sophisticated version of a fraud story. What other options existed for an officer in this special predicament? He couldn't stay at that hotel in London forever. Would the Recess Department eventually have helped him to get home? Should the Police have arrested him, when the hotel manager got tired of having him stay there as a non-paying guest? I thought of all these things while waiting for a new bank loan.

According to the alternative theory, that I alone find quite trustworthy, Anderson was not really a scammer from the start, but a soldier with a muddled economy and with a spacious conscience for financial affairs. I think he was at least partly the one he claimed to be –a soldier stationed in Syria–, I believe he had a less than agreeable time in London, and the same is true of his return home in Baltimore. I believe that he was a lonely man with few friends. Little wonder he was, if he behaved like this to people he met. He gave me misleading information about his finances. He was most likely aware of his tax debts from the beginning of our friendship. In all other respects, he gave me the impression of being an ordinary middle-aged, middle-class American.

The Recess Department is probably an unofficial agency that helps military personnel get free from their service on the field. I suppose that military personnel are not expected to take leave from their service on the field without special and very important reasons. This extra resort that the Recess Department is in charge of, should therefore be paid by the soldiers themselves. This is what I suppose to be true. "There's a lot about the Army that you don't know", Edward had said. I believe he was right in this. There is also a lot about military men's behavior I didn't know.

The existence of a Recess Department was denied by both the Defense Department and the Department of Peacekeeping Operations. Strictly speaking they had just denied that the department existed *within* their organization. They might have known about this unofficial agency, though they didn't admit that.

The email address that the Recess Department used was not consistent. Mostly it was "defencedepartment.com", spelt with a *c*, not *s*, as it should be according to the American way of spelling. On a few occasions –in the first messages from them–, it was "defensedpt.gov", with the American spelling. According to the information on the website of the U.S. Army, messages from a military person should always have a post address ending with *mil*. This supports my theory that the department was working outside of the U.S. Army.

I found many references to scam or fraud when I later contacted different corporations and authorities that somehow were concerned in this business about Anderson. Even the bank officials that I was in touch with during this period seemed to be well familiar with money transactions that were made because of fraud. They sent a letter asking about some of the transactions I had made to bank accounts abroad. They asked for information about the purpose of these transactions, and I admitted that I had probably been targeted for fraud.

In March I received an e-letter from the American Embassy in London. The official who had written the letter, referred to my letter that I had sent one of the first days of January, i.e. more than two months earlier. She assumed that I had been victimized by a swindler, even though I had not suggested that this was the case in my letter. I had asked for their help to make Mr. Anderson, an American citizen abroad, get home, while he was still staying in London, unable to pay for his hotel and flight home. She said there were lots of similar cases, people who had given thousands of dollars to men they didn't know. She advised me to turn to the London police department, the so-called ActionFraud. She also referred to the Federal Bureau of Investigation in the U.S., where I could fill out a form for Cybercrimes. And I did. I spent hours on writing down all details about the transactions of money via the Recess Department, and about all persons being involved in this business.

Anderson and Nelson, but not Maria MacMillan, have called me on the phone a few times. Edward told me she wanted to talk to me when his son had health issues and was transferred to hospital. I assumed she wanted to persuade me to contribute financially to Brian's operation. In her letter to me she stressed that Edward had not given her my email address, he had said "Lisa doesn't want to talk with you, I must have her admission first." She had got the email address from Brian. I mostly refused to answer the phone calls from Edward, and he tried many times to phone me. It was like I always was paralyzed with fear, when he tried to call me. The two phone calls from him that I did accept were very short, there was noise in the background and I was too tense to catch all the words he spoke. Hearing exactly what people *say* on the phone has for some reason always been a problem for me.

I had on both occasions the feeling that he was troubled by something. When I asked him how he was doing he answered "I'm okay" and that phrase is mostly used when you are not feeling happy. It is customary to answer "I'm fine" no matter how you feel. It is of course partly due to the persons involved and the situation. Edward talked to me as if I were a close friend or a sister. His answer was well motivated on both occasions. But I didn't want him to elaborate on his situation. I wanted to finish our conversation as fast as possible. I asked him to write a message instead, which he did. He asked me what telephone number I had on my display when I talked to him on the phone. When I told him, he confirmed it was the correct number.

One characteristic feature that they had in common is of course their asking for more money from me. They all seemed to be flippant about spending money, at least other people's money. Maria MacMillan asked for money on behalf of Anderson and his son. She didn't speak in her own interest and appeared to be more modest in her demands.

When I was contacted by the "barrister" Nelson I was fooled to believe that it really was possible for me to be compensated for the losses. He used a false authority to dupe me. He might have cooperated with the organization who sent the illegitimate notification letters. Their documents appeared to be authentic, the barrister Cindy averred they were. If they were illegitimate, she would be an accomplice.

I have done some research on this type of crimes. Trusting a person is a significant part of fraud. The criminals first gain your confidence, and then use this confidence to ask for money. Sometimes the fraudster makes the victim part of a romantic relationship. Anderson would sometimes in the beginning of our friendship use an intimate note in his way of addressing me with "my love" or "honey". But he changed his way of addressing me, when he learnt that I did not see him as a romantic relationship. He changed to a more modest way of addressing me, more suitable for an ordinary friend or a sister.

Special divisions of the Police are busy investigating this type of crimes in most countries. ActionFraud at the British police and Internet Crime Complaint Center (IC3) at the FBI are those police units that are specialized in these crimes in Great Britain and the United States respectively. Australia's website for this type of crime is called Scamwatch, where Australian citizens can report if they have been victims of scam.

When I read the story about Georgina on the website Scamwatch, I find at least partially a parallel to my case. It says on this website: "Don't transfer money even if the person sounds genuine." I would probably have complied with this advice, had I known more about the situation. It is impossible to tell the difference between honest men and the dishonest ones, if you don't know them personally.

Scam is a wide concept used to encompass all sorts of internet crimes where money transactions are made between the perpetrator and the victim. I found some information about the frequencies of the different types of scam, but it is difficult to estimate the extent of the crime, there is the dark figure of crime. Many persons victimized in this way don't report the crime to the police. They feel embarrassed or ashamed if they have been fooled. Another reason people don't report is the lack of confidence in the police. On Scamwatch's website I found stories from real life to show how these connections are typically established. Several different types of scam are identified, some of which are *unexpected money, unexpected winnings, fake charities* and *dating & romance.* While charity scam usually refers to scam in the backwater of huge accidents that have hit the population of a certain part in the world, e.g. The Katrina storm in the U.S. in 2010 or the Tsunami in Malaysia in 2004, the scam I was exposed for, is a mix of fake charity for one specific person, Edward Anderson, and later the unexpected refund of the money from this "charity", since I first believed Edward was an honest man who needed help in a very troublesome situation, and I believed he was able to pay back on a later occasion. When the barristers and the Recess Department later offered their help, it was a kind of "getting back unexpected money".

The "bad guys" in this story are, or pretend to be, respectable people from Western countries: the U.S. and the UK. Anderson might have used another military person's name and title. He took my economic safety away from me, he didn't care what agonizing situations he exposed me for. He acted in a very egotistical way. Considering the fact that he is, or pretended to be, an officer, his acting in this way was even more blameworthy. It is human to be afraid of dying, it is understandable that you ask for help in an extreme situation like war. But a soldier is expected to endure more than common civil persons. A soldier, in particular an officer, should be able to remain at his post no matter what happens. Edward claimed he was seriously injured, but he probably exaggerated his physical state. He would not have been able to handle deep injuries during the several weeks he stayed in London, had he been badly injured.

I don't know what attitude I should take to the Recess Department and to the U.S. Interpol that sent the notification letters to the barristers Nelson and Flynn. Both the Defense Department and the Department of Peacekeeping Operations within UN denied the existence of a Recess Department within their departments. I have however had so much correspondence with this organization, that it must exist, even if their activity is not officially acknowledged. The document from U.S. Interpol that was sent to me and barrister Flynn, telling me 104,000 euros were reserved for me, was not legitimate according to the Interpol in Washington. I noticed they used another logo on their notification letters than the Interpol in Washington did.

Every time I got a negative answer or no answer at all, I felt extremely depressed. If I had a fortune, I would have invested some money only to get some true facts about this person who deceived me. I would have hired a detective to find out some facts about this man and his life. I never wanted to be a close friend of him, but I was curious about his life experiences. I wanted to know if he was "known by the Police" which is the wording you hear when a person has done something wrong and has done so many times before. It seemed he was disappointed at the American society, since he said that he would like to relocate to another country in Europe. "In America everything you do is monitored" he said once. Even though he lied about his economy and deceived me, I believe that the bulk of the personal information he gave me was true.

I have used other names than the ones that the persons involved have used about themselves. They have caused me serious troubles and depression, but it is still unknown to what extent they have lied about themselves and this matter. It is a fact that they have deprived me of 150,000 euros, but I can't stop having some hopes, however small, that Anderson or the Recess Department will finally give back at least part of the money. I have no hopes whatsoever that the lawyer Nelson will do the right thing and pay back the money he was entrusted with.

THE CONSEQUENCES
FOR MY LIFE

The fraud that I suffered has affected me in several different ways. My economy is ruined, despite my several years of professional work. I haven't calculated how much these loans I took because of Anderson have cost including all the interest and fees that I have paid. The loans amounted to 150,000 euro, a fabulous sum for me. Most of my pension will be reserved for paying back bank loans the next ten years. I don't know how to make it, when the pension I get will be smaller after some years. I have so far paid off about 10% of the debts. If I had lived in the 19th century or further back in time, I had run the risk of being seated in a "guild cabin", a prison for those who could not pay their debts. But I live in a modern society with a social security net for those who do not manage their finances.

I can't help blaming myself for the naïve trust I showed Anderson, for the unreasonably high bank loans I took to appease him when he bothered me with his endless *please please help me.* It gets me that he so many times persuaded me, manipulated me, to do more and more of the same thing – raise money, though I have no fortune to make use of. I thought I was much more sensible, more pragmatic than I appeared to be during these four-five months that I had frequent contacts with him. The fact that he gave me access to a bank account in his name made me feel quite sure that he was able to pay back his loans.

I feel bothered every time I pass by a beggar in my daily life. There are many beggars from East European countries, first and foremost Romania and Bulgaria, in public places, since the borders between the countries belonging to the European Union have been opened according to the Schengen Agreement, that most European countries have signed. I used to give the beggars some coins, or something to eat. I have now a more critical attitude to the life style those people represent. Begging seems to be a way of living for them which they transfer to children and grandchildren. They reportedly prefer begging to doing simple and low-paid jobs.

All adults should do their utmost to earn their living without begging. You are always responsible for your own life and the choices you make as an adult. That's what I told Edward once when he was asking for more money. He wanted to make me responsible for his well-being, which was quite absurd. There may be hard times, unemployment, or a bad government in your country, but you must take on the main responsibility for your own life and the lives of your children.

The beggars sometimes put up a notice with some information about themselves, their (bad) health status, or about the purpose of collecting money this way. The women usually say they have 2–5 children to support, the men say they need money to "walk" back to Romania. They claim to be seriously ill, having diabetes or cardiac problems. They write their information in a faulty Swedish or English, written with letters that are childishly imperfect. The women's information about their children –with pictures of their pretty children– enhances their message. Who would deny a hungry child food? Especially women are supposed to heed warm feelings towards all children, not only their own ones. But as time goes by, we tend to get more insensitive to all those appeals. The beggars remind me of Anderson's numerous *please please please.*

Even more serious is maybe the loss of confidence in my fellow human beings. I have lost my trust in military personnel, all authorities, corporations and human beings generally. I have received so much information, full of contradictions, from all kinds of sources. I don't trust people who try to convince me I should do this or that. My experiences have taught me I should beware of all people who keep saying "Trust me" – because in most cases you can't trust them at all! You have to rely on your own reason, even though it is not perfectly safe either. My self-esteem has been seriously injured. I am usually not one to be seduced by advertisements for commodities I don't need, I don't gamble and I am usually skeptical towards salespersons. Yet I was victimized by some fraudsters.

If I had heard anyone else tell me about an experience like this, I would probably have considered that person to be credulous, not capable of making a good judgement. For my defense, I can refer to the general need to be kind, do something good for other people, that I suppose most people feel. Even those who have no religious faith at all seem to encompass values that are the essence of Christianity. Empathy implies understanding other people's feelings and actions, and a natural consequence of understanding their situation is to help them if necessary. Empathy is probably an indispensable quality for humans to survive in the long run. We can't help ourselves in all kinds of situations, we are more or less dependent on each other. But values like *honesty, respect* and *fairness* are not values that are unanimously cherished by all humans. The core meaning of these words, i.e. what deeds and behavior really agree with these values, is not a matter of course, and is not even important to all individuals. There would be peace on earth, if everyone thought that killing or harassing other humans is absolutely wrong. There would be fewer divorces if everyone considered infidelity to be totally wrong and acted accordingly. There would be no frauds or thefts if everyone deemed this incongruent with basic respect for other human individuals. A crime like this –fraud– is a cardinal sin for lawyers in particular.

I felt pity for a man who was in a difficult situation, seriously hurt according to himself, and most likely depressed. He seemed to be very lonely. My life feels more meaningful if I do something that matters for other people. This altruistic feeling is something basic to humankind. We are sociable, we need other people and to this end we are ready to sacrifice something that in short sight may cause us trouble but in the long run will make our life better. It is difficult to know how far we should go in our sacrifices. "You should love your neighbor as much as yourself" the Bible says. This means also that you must take care of yourself as much as of other humans. Most people confine themselves to a small amount of money, if anything at all. You give some coins in the collection-box, or make a payment to a charitable organization on some occasions, you buy things at a market in favor of a special category. If you have suffered from a severe disease, or one of your dear ones has, you are inclined to sponsor research on this disease. Most people have come across difficult situations, and most of them are grateful to have escaped death thanks to medical care. The problem is that some less conscientious people take advantage of this willingness to help. They feign a pitiful situation and appeal to our willingness to help them out of this situation, or at least to alleviate it. They use more or less sophisticated tricks to dupe you. Sometimes it may be easy to see through their tricks. I tried to break away from the cheaters on some points but was persuaded to go on, and this will always bother me. I know there are many people who have made the same mistake, but knowing that is a poor consolation.

After all the troubles I have gone through, I don't feel like giving anything at all to strangers. I saw a stranger as a friend I didn't know before this experience. Now I'm well aware that he or she may be an enemy, someone who doesn't care if my own life is ruined by helping them. The dishonesty and greediness from these people I have been in touch with have somehow ruined my willingness to give anything to unknown corporations and people! I suffer from compassion fatigue. That is the consequence of feeling abused, swindled. Bad acts spread bitterness, hate to other people. You feel so humiliated by a swindler that it destroys every bit of trust in strangers.

There is a characteristic trait of humans and animals alike: to make a big division line between US and THEM. THEY are the strangers, whom you don't know anything about but who might be dangerous to your own kind. Biologists usually point to the animal within us, the reptile brain works in many situations when we are exposed to stress. Animals and humans alike want to spread their genes, partly by restricting other individuals from spreading their genes. This leads to hostility between different flocks of animals of the same species. In some respects, we behave like animals. I venture to say we are much worse. Animals kill other animals of their own species to survive, they protect their territories against individuals who don't belong to their own flock. Humans kill or hurt other people for many other dubious reasons.

I have asked myself if I would ask for money from my neighbors, friends or relatives if I were in a similar situation as Edward was. It seemed okay for him to ask for money from me, though we knew each other only superficially. We had chatted via Facebook for a couple of weeks, when he asked for my help. And he kept asking for my help, no matter how much was needed for different purposes and despite my worries about my economy.

Would I ask some friend, in particular a Facebook friend, for money, if I were staying in a place I hated and wanted to get away from? My answer is definitely NO. I would never ask for money, especially not this size of amounts, that Edward asked for. I never asked my parents for financial help, even when I was badly off. They gave me financial support over my first 30 years, and I have of course supported my own adult son in some situations. This is a matter of course within a family. But not when it comes to people outside the family. I took a pride to be economically independent, even towards my husband. This is very important for the equity between men and women. I have lost the feeling of being independent and "safe" that I had before this happened.

I don't know exactly what the situation was like for Edward. Had he suffered severely from pains, before asking for my help? He never complained of bad health after he had left the camp, but according to the lawyer Nelson, he was in a bad shape after staying first in the custody, then at a hotel in London for some weeks.

I have been mentally ill, and I have not yet recovered from the extreme strains to my psychic health I suffered. I will not be able to trust a stranger another time. I am ashamed to say so, having been a guardian for so many young persons from other countries. I used to stand up for people in distress, I still want to do so. But I will be much more restrictive, I will no more take honesty for granted with people I don't know very well.

When I was a patient at the psychiatric clinic I was diagnosed with *crisis reaction*, later *depression* was added. I met some doctors and nurses who helped me to recover from the worst effects of my experiences. I take medicines for depression and sleeping problems. The most important thing for people who have been through a crisis is to focus on something they are committed to. I am still interested in learning more about my fellow human beings, though from a larger distance than before. It is an ironic fact that my curiosity about other people, the compassion with people in distress has led to misery for myself. I thought Facebook would be used as a communication canal between individuals from different cultures, with all kinds of religions and interests. A Facebook account could work as a medium for friendships of a different kind, as pen friends used to be before the advent of Internet. A friendship that was restricted to the written media, not a physical contact. Now I realize the risks of having these more or less anonymous friends. While a pen friend is always connected to a definite address and name, a Facebook friend can be anyone but the one he or she claims to be. The police warn you not to accept friendships on Facebook from people you haven't met in real life. This is contrary to the original idea of having a broad contact net on Facebook. You must protect your safety from strangers who want to harm you in some way, no matter if it concerns your identity, your private life or your finances. I nowadays reject all requests from people I am not familiar with.

All adults have to take responsibility for their own lives, not put the responsibility on somebody else or society in general. This is my cardinal rule. I have been gullible, but that is not a crime. I wanted to do something good. Still, I cannot help feeling very ashamed of my acting against common sense. I thought I was sensible and careful enough to avoid making mistakes like the ones I actually did. Now I know I am not. I am not a weak person, I am a soft person.

Crisis is a word that has been described as "change", you have lost something, but you can replace it with something else, perhaps something more valuable in the long run. You are not the same person after the crisis as before. I believed that I could see the difference between good and bad people. I cannot. Or – rather – there are so many shades of black that you don't know when the black shades predominate over the white. My view of this story is that Edward chose to pull me down into this misery because he himself was in a very difficult situation as a soldier in a war zone. He must have been aware of his debts, but he probably thought that I would be "cool" enough to take the loss of money without grumble. Or he was an unscrupulous cheater from the very start…

I will go on living my life, though my economy sets very tight frames for my activities. I will have some difficult moments when I think of all that I lost, I will regret everything I had to go through because a man in another country asked for my help. But I will think of all the good things that I still can enjoy. Unlike most young boys and girls I have been in touch with these last years I live in a country with peace; we have not been directly involved in a war for two hundred years. Our neighbor countries, Denmark, Norway and Finland were all occupied or directly involved in World War II. Unlike so many peoples on our earth, we live in a democratic country with all the benefits it implies.

I live in a very peaceful and beautiful place. I enjoy the possibility to hear the sound of water from the rapid nearby, I enjoy the twitter of birds, I love to see deer, foxes and on some rare occasion elks outside my window. I am able to turn off my cell phone, my computer and just listen to the sounds from nature.

Printed in the United States
By Bookmasters